The Complete Book of
Papercraft

The Complete Book of
Papercraft

OVER 50 DESIGNS FOR
HANDMADE PAPER, CARDS, GIFT-WRAPPING,
DECOUPAGE, AND MANIPULATING PAPER

LYNNE GARNER

 ST. MARTIN'S GRIFFIN

NEW YORK

For Trudi

THE COMPLETE BOOK OF PAPERCRAFT. Copyright © 2006 by Breslich & Foss Ltd.
All rights reserved. Printed in China. No part of this book may be used or
reproduced in any manner whatsoever without written permission except in
the case of brief quotations embodied in critical articles or reviews. For
information, address St. Martin's Press, 175 Fifth Avenue, New York, N.Y.
10010.

www.stmartins.com

Text by Lynne Garner
Photographs by Shona Wood
Design by Janet James

Library of Congress Cataloging-in-Publication Data Available Upon Request

ISBN-10: 0-312-35953-5
ISBN-13: 978-0-312-35953-9

First published in the United Kingdom by Breslich & Foss Ltd.

First U.S. Edition: November 2006

10 9 8 7 6 5 4 3 2 1

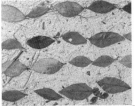

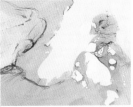

contents

Introduction

Today we take paper for granted because it is all around us. We use paper in the form of newspapers and books, we wrap our gifts in paper, we hang paper on our walls, we eat off paper and—even in this age of plastic—we still use paper notes to buy many of the things we need.

The history of paper spans many centuries and many continents. The first form of paper was invented over 5,000 years ago. It was on the banks of the Nile River in Egypt that a local plant called *Cyperus papyrus* was used to create a paper known as "papyrus." To make it, the stem of the plant was soaked, cut into strips, layered, pounded into thin sheets, then dried in the sun. Once in its dried form it could be rolled, carried around easily and would, if kept in the right conditions, last for centuries.

However, the method of paper-making used today is traditionally attributed to the Chinese inventor T'sai Lun in the years around 105 AD. He is recorded as having experimented with many materials, including bark, hemp, and even fishing net.

To make his paper, T'sai Lun soaked the fibers in a large vat of water, then placed a screen in the water that caught the fibers in a thin sheet when the screen was lifted out. This new method was to change the way paper was made forever.

The spread of paper-making was a slow process and it wasn't until the Chinese were at war with the Islamic world in the 8th century that paper journeyed further West. During the course of a battle, several Chinese papermakers were captured and their skills adopted. Paper eventually made it to Europe in the 12th century, when Spain and Portugal were invaded by Arabs from North Africa, who brought the secret of paper-making with them. Until this time parchment (made from animal skin) had been used in Europe, but this was an expensive medium. As printing technology developed in the Renaissance, so did the need for more and more paper. Eventually, the fibers from trees were discovered to be an ideal and cheap source, and trees remain the favorite raw material to this day.

Nowadays, paper is produced to suit the specific needs of its many end users: the watercolorist who wants paper to paint upon; the scrapbooker who needs acid free papers; the quiller who demands paper that will hold its form once twisted; and—last but not least—you the papercrafter, who is eager to mix any form of paper or card stock to create interesting and innovative craft projects. And that's where this book fits in. Using a wide variety of craft techniques, I hope to inspire you to create fun and exciting projects ranging from simple greeting cards and wrapping paper to photograph frames and gift boxes. Turn the pages and discover the joys of this versatile medium.

Lynne Garner

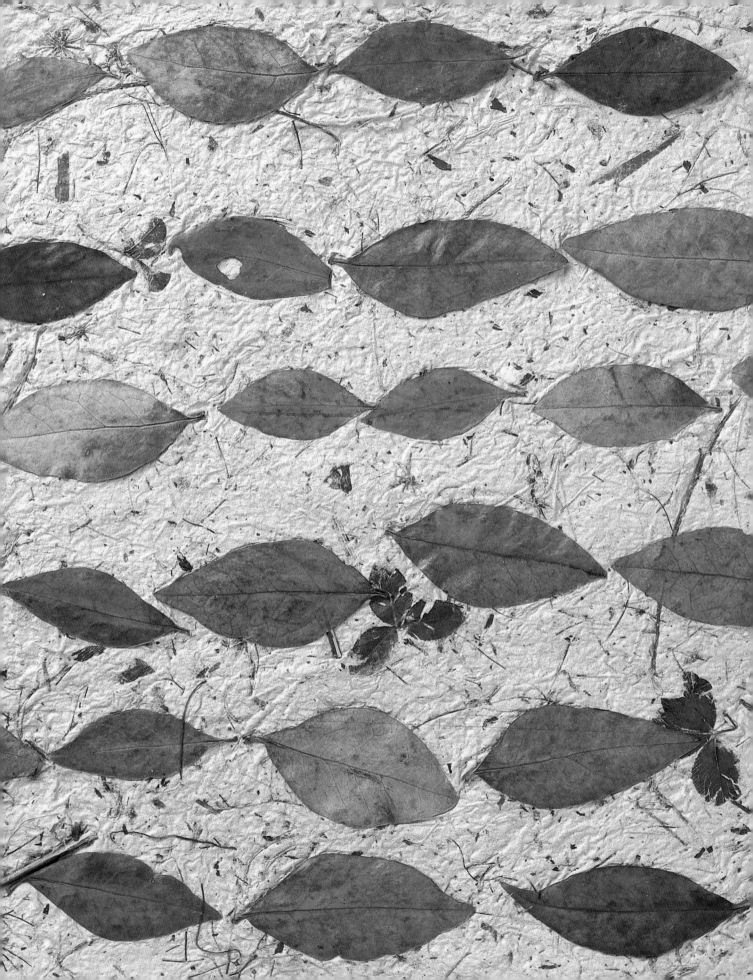

CHAPTER ONE

Creating Handmade Paper

Making your own paper is not as difficult as you might imagine, and it's great fun. It also opens up all kinds of possibilities for recycling, allowing you to create individual projects from "waste" materials such as shredded paper and roses that have dried but kept their beauty. Different paper pulp mixtures will result in different papers, and even those that don't turn out quite as planned will have their own charm!

Making a mold and deckle

The mold and deckle are rectangular frames of the same size: the mold has wire mesh stretched across it, and the deckle is a frame with no mesh. Although molds and deckles can be purchased ready made, they can be expensive. To keep costs down, make your own by following the instructions below.

YOU WILL NEED

screwdriver

8 L-shaped aluminum braces

2 plain wooden picture frames

16 brass screws (short enough not to go all the way through the frame)

thick gloves

wire cutters or strong scissors (suitable for cutting the wire mesh)

aluminum wire mesh (available from car accessory shops)

hammer

brass nails

1. Use the screwdriver to attach the L-shaped braces to each corner of both frames with the brass screws. This will strengthen the frames, which will be constantly going in and out of water.

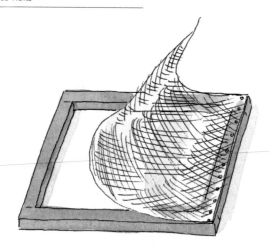

2. Protecting you hands with the gloves, cut the wire mesh to the same size as the picture frame. Using the hammer, nail the wire mesh in place on the back of one of the picture frames. This will be your mold.

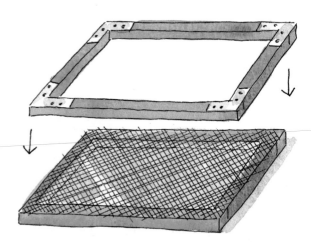

3. To use, place the empty frame (the deckle) on top of the one with the mesh attached (the mold), sandwiching the mesh between the two frames.

Making a basic paper mixture

Many types of material can be used to create your own handmade paper, from recycled office paper to newspaper, brown wrapping paper, junk mail, envelopes, and even tissue paper. Once you have made the paper pulp, keep it in a cool place and use it within a few days.

YOU WILL NEED

paper

large bowl (for soaking)

large cup or mug

blender

large container

1. Rip the paper into small pieces about 1 in. (2.5 cm) or 2 in. (5 cm) square.

2. Place the paper in the large bowl then pour over enough boiling water to cover the paper scraps and allow some movement. Let soak overnight to allow the fibers to separate.

3. Take one cup of soaked paper to three cups of cold water and place in the blender. Turn the blender to high speed and liquidize for a minute, or until the paper is completely broken down and the pulp is a smooth, creamy consistency.

4. Pour the pulp into a large container ready for the making of your paper. Continue in this fashion until you have the required amount of paper pulp for your project.

TIPS

- If you have a thick paper that will not break down by soaking alone, place the paper and water mixture in a large rustproof saucepan and simmer on the stove for half an hour before soaking for four hours.

- Change the color of your paper by mixing different types together. For example, plain white paper can be mixed with brown wrapping paper to make something that has a more natural or "ethnic" look.

- Use the paper pulp within a couple of days. It can go bad and begin to smell if left longer, especially during hot spells.

- While using the blender, listen to the sound of the motor: turn it off if it sounds strained.

How to use a mold and deckle

Before you begin to make a sheet of paper, prepare a "couching mat" for Step 5 by laying a wet, lint-free kitchen cloth on a board. The cloth must be wet: if you place the wet pulp on a dry cloth it may shrink or stretch out of shape.

YOU WILL NEED

mold and deckle

deep, flat-bottomed plastic container (large enough to take mold and deckle comfortably)

paper pulp mixture

wooden spoon

3 lint-free kitchen cloths

board at least 2 in. (5 cm) bigger all around than the mold and deckle

sponge

indoor washing line (best hung over a bath or similar)

clothes pegs or pins

newspaper

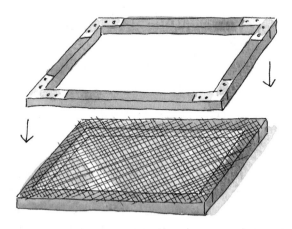

1. Place the deckle over the mold, keeping the mesh side uppermost. Fill the container with paper pulp to a level at least 3 in. (8 cm) below the edge of the container, or the liquid might splash out when you raise the frame.

2. Stir the pulp vigorously with the spoon, then immediately plunge the short side of the frame vertically into the container. In one smooth movement, tilt the frame into a horizontal position and hold it flat under the water.

3. Still holding the frame flat, bring it up to the surface of the water, gently shaking it from side to side and from front to back. This will ensure the pulp is spread evenly across the entire frame.

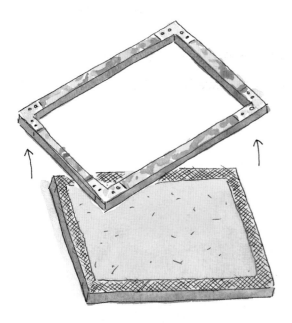

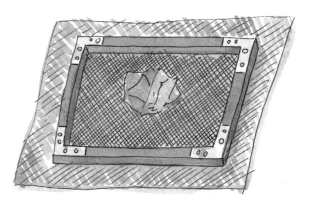

4. Lift the frame out of the water, keeping it flat, and let the water drain back into the container. Place the mold carefully on a flat surface and lift the deckle away. Make sure no drips fall onto the pulp, as these could cause holes in the paper.

5. When most of the water has drained away, carefully turn the mold paper-side down and lay it flat on the couching mat. Blot the paper through the mesh with a dry sponge, absorbing as much water as possible to form a vacuum between the board, the pulp, and the mesh. Lift the corners of the cloth from the board to release the vacuum and carefully remove the mold. Should you find the paper is still stuck to the mesh, blot again then flip over and carefully remove the kitchen cloth from the frame, lifting one corner of the cloth at a time.

TIPS

- To speed the drying process, the paper can be ironed dry. This also has the benefit of creating a paper that is slightly thinner than one created by hanging it up to dry. Iron the paper between two pieces of fine cotton fabric so the paper does not stick to the iron's base plate.

- To make sheets of paper that are larger than your deckle, lay out a large piece of fine cotton cloth. Then, rather than hanging the paper to dry, place each piece on the cotton cloth overlapping the edges slightly. Press over the surface with a sponge to remove excess water and let dry.

6. Lift the damp kitchen cloth with the paper attached and pin it to an indoor clothes line. If you are worried about whatever is beneath the line, place sheets of newspaper beneath it to catch the drips. When almost dry, place the sheet of paper between two dry kitchen cloths and under a pile of heavy books, so it dries flat.

Adding plant material to handmade paper

Some lovely patterns can be achieved by adding plant material such as leaves, flower heads, and petals to the paper pulp. To make these papers, either add the leaves and petals directly to a very fine pulp, or drop them onto the pulp just after lifting the frame from the container in Step 4 of "How to use a mold and deckle" on page 15. This method gives you more control over how the petals are distributed than if you add them to the liquid. Items that can be added to the pulp include:

- Rose petals
- Flower heads
- Leaves
- Grasses

Adding color to handmade paper

Another way to add interest to handmade paper is to introduce color by using natural ingredients, such as vegetables. Onion skins will dye the paper yellow, while chunks of beet will give it a strong purple color. Chop the desired vegetable into small pieces and place them in the food processor with the paper pulp as described in Step 3 of "Making a basic paper mixture" on page 13. Take care when working with colored pulp to protect your clothes with an apron and wear rubber or latex gloves to save your hands from being stained as well!

For a simple but stunning variation, make paper with different colored sides. Make up two batches of paper pulp in different colors, making one slightly thicker than the other. Create a sheet of paper from the thicker pulp following Steps 1–5 of "How to use a mold and deckle" on pages 14–15, then dip the deckle into the second container of thinner paper pulp and repeat the process. In Step 5, place the second sheet on top of the first and blot off before hanging the paper to dry. Blotting will stick the second sheet to the first, giving you a piece of paper that is a different color on each side.

Left: Beet juice added to a leaf paper gives it a gorgeous purple color.

Adding fragrance to handmade paper

During the paper-making process, scent can be added in the form of essential oils. Alternatively, place sheets of homemade or store-bought paper in a plastic bag with a potpourri sachet and leave for two or three weeks while the paper absorbs the scent. Try some of these natural papers:

- Lavender-scented paper
- Lemon-scented paper
- Rose-scented paper

Right: Turn a sheet of scented paper into an envelope by unfolding an existing one and tracing around it to give you the pattern. Fold the paper to make your own fragrant envelope.

Below: Fragrant handmade paper tied up in ribbon makes a perfect, vintage-style gift.

Adding pattern
to handmade paper

All kinds of paper items and similar things can be added to
handmade paper. Tear or cut larger pieces—such as candy
wrappers—into small strips, then mix some of these in with
the paper pulp when you pour it into the container in Step 1,
and sprinkle others directly onto the pulp after lifting the
frame from the container in Step 4 of "How to use a mold
and deckle" on page 15.

Things you can use include:

- Gold stars
- Metallic foil
- Candy wrappers
- Metallic glitter
- Colored glitter
- Confetti
- Wrapping paper

Making papier-mâché

If you have any paper pulp left over after making up a batch of handmade paper, it can be used to create papier-mâché. Papier-mâché is great for adding embellishments to your papercraft projects, or giving texture to plain surfaces, such as the picture frame shown below.

YOU WILL NEED

wooden spoon

leftover paper pulp

sieve

bowl

non-toxic white craft glue

rubber or latex gloves

1. With the wooden spoon, press the leftover paper pulp through a sieve to remove most of the water. Discard the water and place the pulp in a clean bowl. Add a drop of glue to the pulp and mix well with the spoon.

2. Put on the gloves, then squeeze out the excess moisture and apply the gluey mixture to the surface you want to decorate, building up layers until you achieve the desired effect.

3. Leave the papier-mâché to dry overnight before painting or adding other surface embellishments.

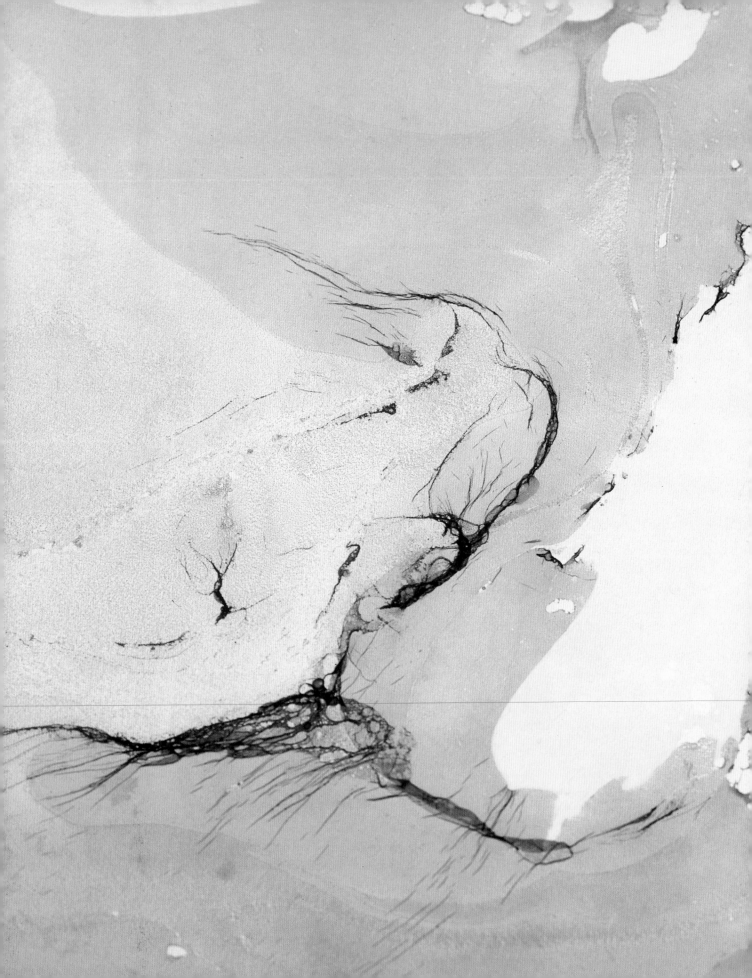

CHAPTER TWO

Decorating Paper

This part of the book sets out fun ideas for decorating both handmade and store-bought paper and cardstock stock that you can transform into greeting cards, gift boxes, wrapping paper, and more. None of the techniques in this section is complicated or expensive, so experiment and have fun!

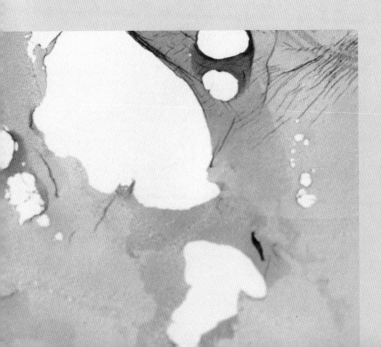

Making and using stamps

There are any number of ways to make stamps, which can then be used to decorate your individual projects. As school kids, many of us made stamps by carving potatoes, but few of us would think of using such humble ingredients now we are adults! However, root vegetables and some fruit can be used to create bold patterns. Keep the shape simple and graphic: for example, you might like to try one of the heart templates from page 148.

YOU WILL NEED

white paper

black marker pen

potato

sharp knife

paper towels

scissors

newspaper

paint

old plate

1. Draw your design on a piece of paper with the black marker pen, making sure the shape is no larger than the surface of the potato you are using.

2. Cut the potato in half and blot the surface with a paper towel to remove excess moisture. With the scissors, cut out the paper design and trace around it onto the surface of the potato.

3. Carefully cut around the design with a sharp knife, removing a layer approximately $1/4$ in. (5 mm) thick.

4. Lay the paper you wish to decorate on a layer of newspapers to protect your work surface. Tip some paint onto the plate and dip the potato stamp into it, then press the potato down on the paper. When you are happy with the design, leave it to dry.

> **TIP**
>
> • Other fruits and vegetables can be used to make stamps. For example, an apple cut in half across the middle gives you a circle with a small star (where the pips are), and a pepper cut in half makes a pretty design that looks like a tulip.

More ideas for stamping

A variety of hard surfaces can be used to print from, including linoleum blocks and erasers. Draw a simple design on the surface of the eraser then cut away around the design with a lino-cutting tool to a depth of about ¼ in. (5 mm). Lines can also be carved into the surface, but don't make them too shallow or they will get filled with paint. If you use a block of linoleum (shown below), glue it to several squares of thick cardstock to make it deep enough to handle.

To make a stamp that creates a softer image, recycle an old mouse mat. Mats can be cut and mounted in the same way as the linoleum version, but use a craft knife instead of a lino-cutting tool. Ink up your new "stamps" and get printing!

SAFETY TIP

- Always cut away from you, making sure your hands are kept out of the way of the knife blade or lino-cutting tool.

Making a stencil

Stenciling is a simple technique that requires few tools. Stencils can be used to apply surface decoration and to create pressure-embossed designs, giving you two looks for the price of one. Inspiration for stencil designs can be found everywhere, including clip art on your computer; art books; fancy food packaging, such as Easter egg boxes; carpet or wallpaper designs, and store-bought rubber stamps.

YOU WILL NEED

design to copy

tracing paper

pencil

cutting mat

stencil acetate

masking tape

craft knife

1. Place your chosen design beneath the tracing paper and trace the design onto the paper with the pencil, bearing in mind where the "bridges" of the stencil should be. Bridges are the narrow pieces, about $1/8$ in. (3 mm) in thickness, that break the image into smaller sections and allow you to create lines within the design.

2. Place the completed, traced design on the cutting mat, and lay the acetate film over it. Tape in position with the masking tape. Carefully cut out each section, taking care not to cut into the bridges.

Above: Use a rose stencil to turn plain napkins into pretty table decorations. Be sparing with the ink, so it doesn't sink too far into the napkin.

TIPS

- Avoid designs that use too many small shapes, as these are difficult to cut out.

- Make the bridges at least $1/8$ in. (3 mm) thick and keep them the same thickness throughout the whole design.

- Make sure the bridges between each section are as straight as possible. They are less likely to get caught and bent if they are straight.

Below: Decorate a baby book or scrapbook page with adorable footprints! Keep the surface uneven for a spontaneous effect.

Using a stencil to add color

When you have created your stencil, there are two decorative methods you can use. The first is adding color; the second is pressure-embossing.

YOU WILL NEED

masking tape

stencil

paper or cardstock to decorate

small sponge (cosmetic sponges are ideal)

color ink pads

1. Use small strips of masking tape to fix the stencil over the paper or cardstock you intend to decorate. Dab the sponge onto the surface of the ink pad then use a dabbing motion to transfer the color to the paper or cardstock through the stencil. Be sparing with the ink so it does not run under the stencil.

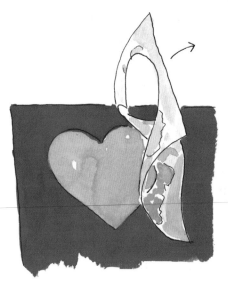

2. When you are happy with the design, carefully remove the masking tape and lift the stencil off the decorated surface.

TIPS

- To get the feel of this technique, practice first on a piece of scrap paper before beginning a project.

- You do not have to create a solid block of color and sometimes it is more interesting to leave the center of the stencil clear.

- Experiment with different colors, blending them together by working one color over another, starting with the lighter colors.

- Try color graduation: place similar colors next to each other, overlapping slightly.

- If creating a layered design, work from the top down so you do not smudge the ink.

- When working on a two-color image, such as a rose with leaves, mask the part of the stencil you are not using to avoid contaminating it with the wrong shade.

- Keep baby wipes handy to clean your stencil between colors.

Right: These examples from "Celebration time" (page 86) demonstrate the different effects produced by pressure-embossing (*above*) and adding color with chalks (*below*).

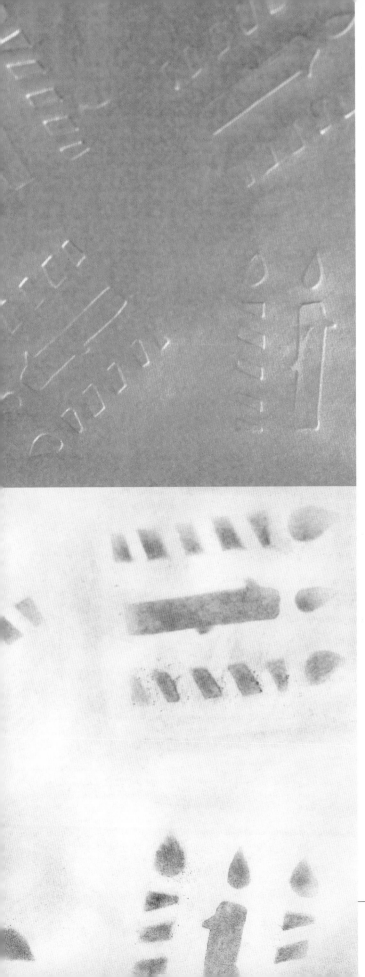

Using a stencil for pressure-embossing

To pressure-emboss a design without a light box, tape your paper to a closed window and use daylight to help you see the stencil beneath.

YOU WILL NEED

stencil

light box (optional)

masking tape

thin cardstock

embossing tool

1. Place the stencil on a light box or window pane and fix it in place with strips of masking tape.

2. Lay the piece of cardstock over the stencil and fix this in place with more masking tape.

3. Trace around the outside edges of the design with the embossing tool, keeping up the same pressure as you would when writing. If you press too hard, the embossing tool will rip the paper; if you press too softly, it will not indent the paper enough to create the effect you are after.

TIPS

- If the embossing tool sticks when going around the stencil, rub the tip of the tool over a sheet of waxed paper.
- Invest in a set of embossing tools that have different-sized tips so you can pick a suitable tip for the paper you are working on. A brittle paper benefits from being embossed with a larger tip, for example, as this is gentler on the paper fibers.
- When pressure-embossing words, remember to place the words back to front. Otherwise your text will be the wrong way around when you turn it over.

Marbling

Marbling is great fun to do, because the results are completely unpredictable! Tools are easy to obtain and are relatively cheap. For best results, use specialized marbling paint, which is oil based, and limit yourself to two or three colors. A limited number of colors tends to create the most striking effects. Before you begin, spread out a layer of newspapers on which to dry the marbled paper in Step 4.

YOU WILL NEED

large, flat-bottomed container

paintbrushes or pipettes

marbling paint

spoon or stick

paper to marble

newspapers

Above: To embellish pencils with scraps of marbled paper, cut the paper to length and fix to the pencils with craft glue.

TIPS

- Wear rubber gloves unless you want marbled fingertips as well!
- Read the instructions on the paints: some require a water softener to be added before marbling can take place.
- To create a feathered pattern, dribble the color back and forth across the bowl. Then, drag a wide-toothed comb across the lines of color.

1. Pour cold water into the container to a depth of about 1 in. (2.5 cm). Using a paintbrush or pipette, drop a little of the marbling paint into the container so it spreads over the surface of the water. Add a second or third color, allowing patterns to form.

2. If the color stays in a solid block on the surface, gently blow until it breaks up and travels across the surface of the water or use a spoon or stick to swirl the paint around.

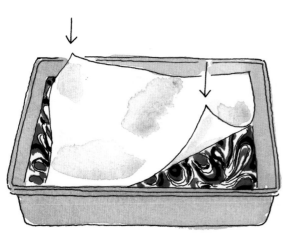

3. When you see a pattern you like, lay the paper on the surface of the water holding two opposite corners and lowering the center of the paper first.

4. The pigment will adhere to the paper. Carefully lift the paper away from the surface and place it paint side up on a layer of newspapers to dry.

Sponging

Sponging is a method that is often used to decorate walls, but it can also be helpful when you want to create a background effect suitable for paper-crafting projects. All you need is a natural sponge, some paint, and a disposable plate. Pour the paint onto the plate, dip the sponge into the paint, then dab off the excess on the side of the plate or on a piece of scrap paper. Dab the paint onto the paper or cardstock you wish to decorate, turning the sponge between each dab and working in a random manner so no pattern appears. If you want to use two or more shades, let the first color dry before adding the second over the top.

Spattering

Spattering is a quick and easy way to achieve interesting results on papers that can then be used on a variety of projects. Before you begin, cover your clothes with an apron and protect your work surface with a wide layer of newspaper because the paint will fly everywhere. Keep some newspaper to one side for drying the finished paper in Step 3.

YOU WILL NEED

newspaper

poster paint, ink, or watercolors

disposable plate or shallow bowl

stiff-bristled paintbrush

rubber or latex gloves

paper to decorate

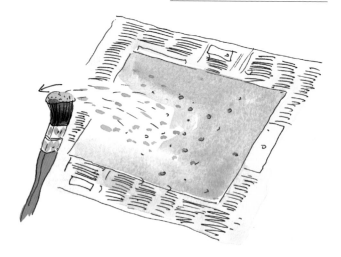

1. Cover your work surface with newspaper, then place a small amount of paint or ink on the plate or in the bowl and add a little water if necessary. The paint should not be too thick or it won't spatter; if it is too thin, it will run. Dip the ends of the bristles in the paint.

2. Put on the gloves then flick the paint onto the surface of the paper, covering as thinly or as thickly as desired.

3. If using more than one color, clean the paintbrush with water and repeat Step 2 with your second color. When you are happy with the pattern, lay the paper on a sheet of newspaper and let dry.

TIPS

- Practice spattering on scrap paper before you start, to make sure the paint is the right consistency.

- If you use your thumb to flick the paint, you'll get a mist of droplets.

Using spattered paper

Spattering is a good method to choose when you want to cover a large sheet of paper, such as the one used here to jazz up a plain notebook.

YOU WILL NEED

book to cover

spattered paper

pencil

ruler

craft knife

cutting board

double-sided tape

scissors

teaspoon

1. Open the book and place it face down on the wrong side of the spattered paper. Cut around the book, leaving a margin of about 1 in. (2.5 cm).

2. Turn over the open book and place it—front cover down—on the wrong side of the paper. Fold the paper into the two corners of the book front and fix in place with double-sided tape. Fold over the outside edges and fix in the same way. Hold the book open at 90 degrees (to allow for the spine) and fix the paper to the back cover in the same way.

3. If the book is a hardcover, close it and make a vertical snip either side of the spine at the top and bottom of the book. Tuck the pieces of paper down into the spine with the back of a teaspoon. Fold over the top and bottom edges of the spattered paper and fix in place with more tape. If the book is a paperback, trim top and bottom of the spattered paper flush with the edges.

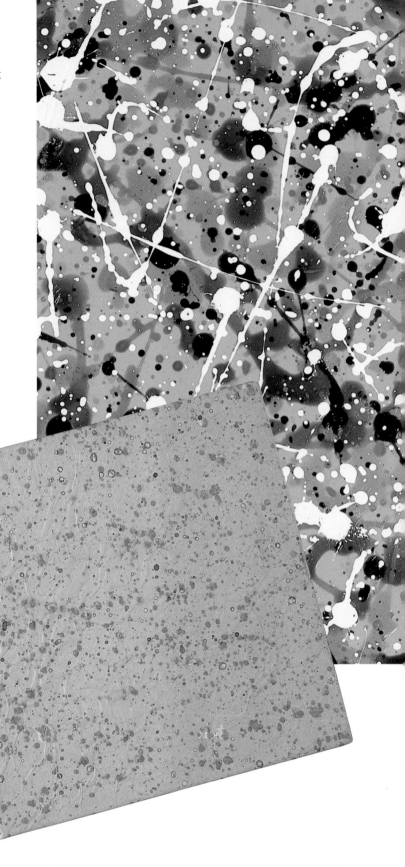

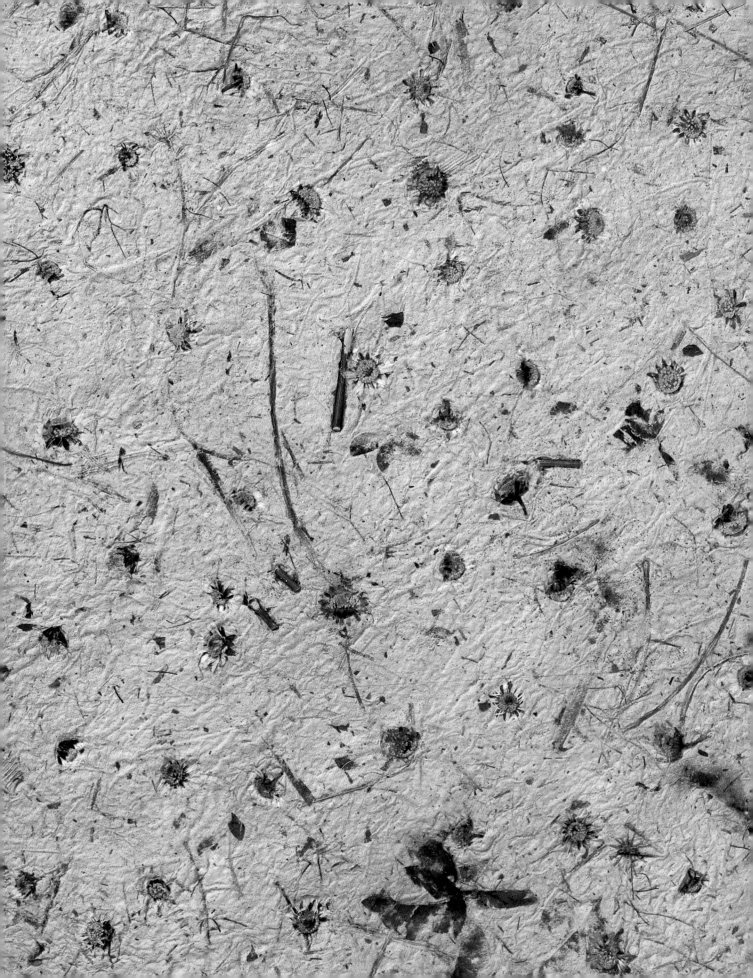

CHAPTER THREE

Stationery and Gift-Wrapping

In this section you will discover how to transform handmade and decorated papers into a range of boxes, tags, and gift-wrapping to suit events from weddings to birthday parties. You'll also find ideas for simple place settings that will add a touch of elegance to family meals.

Music box

With some simple folding and cutting, a square of paper can be turned into a box that is ideal for holding small gifts, such as earrings or cufflinks. The template has the folds marked on it. By using this, you can turn a range of papers into distinctive boxes. We chose music manuscript, but you can use old maps, magazines pages, or scrapbooking paper.

YOU WILL NEED

template from page 138

craft knife

cutting mat

ruler

pencil

two 12 x 8 ^{1}/$_4$ in. (30 x 21 cm) sheets of music manuscript

1 Cut the paper into two squares, making one ^{1}/$_{16}$ in. (2 mm) smaller than the other. (The larger piece will become the lid.) Take the smaller of the two pieces of paper and—on the wrong side—find the middle by drawing two diagonal lines across the center and mark with the pencil.

2 Fold all four corners into the middle then open them out again (marked fold 1 on the template).

3 Fold all the corners to the line marked 1 then unfold them again to make the fold marked 2 on the template.

4 Fold the first corner over to the fold marked 1 on the opposite corner, then unfold. Repeat this action with the other three corners to make the folds marked 4.

5 Following the photograph, cut along one of the folds marked 3 to the point where it meets the next fold marked 3.

6 By turning the paper 90 degrees and repeating the process three more times, you will end up with four cuts as shown above.

7 Fold one corner in twice following the creases made in Steps 2, 3, and 4. Turn the paper 90 degrees and repeat the process.

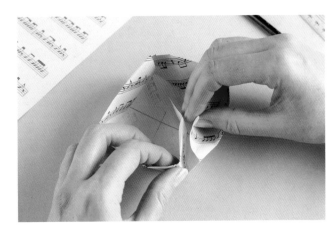

8 Lift each folded section and tuck the pointed end under its neighbor, then fold the second section back down again. This will hold the ends in place.

9 Repeat the process until you have worked around the whole of the box. When complete, repeat Steps 1–9 to make the box lid.

By using scrapbooking paper like that shown here, you can create a huge assortment of boxes in all manner of themes and colors. Seal your box with a matching ribbon for an extra touch of luxury.

V A R I A T I O N

From the heart

To make truly individual boxes why not use a little of your own marbled paper? Marbling is quick and easy and you'll find detailed instructions on pages 30–31. It doesn't matter how many of these pretty boxes you make and decorate because no two marbled papers are ever the same.

YOU WILL NEED

store-bought, heart-shaped box

12 x 8 ¼ in. (30 x 21 cm) sheet of marbled paper

pencil

ruler

scissors

dry glue stick

self-adhesive ribbon

1 Trace around the box lid on the wrong side of the marbled paper with a pencil, then cut out a heart shape, approximately ½ in. (12 mm) larger all around than the template you have drawn. Cut out a long strip of marbled paper making it approximately ½ in. (12 mm) deeper and longer than the lid edge. Cut out a second heart shape and a strip for the box base in the same way.

2 Cover the surface of the lid with glue and place it in the middle of the marbled paper, on the wrong side. With the scissors, snip into the overlapping ½ in. (12 mm) of paper, right up to the outer edge of the lid.

3 Apply glue to the lid edge, then carefully fold down the snipped paper to stick it in place.

4 Cover the lip of the lid (which is now partly covered with paper) with glue and position the paper strip so the edge is flush with the surface of the lid. Stick down all the way around, overlapping the ends slightly.

5 Apply glue to the inside edge of the lid, then snip into the overlapping $1/2$ in. (12 mm) of paper and fold it over the edge so it sticks in place. Repeat Steps 2–5 to decorate the base.

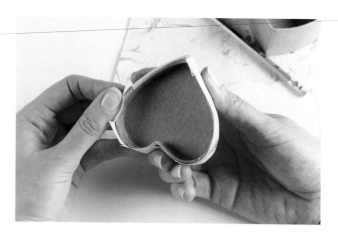

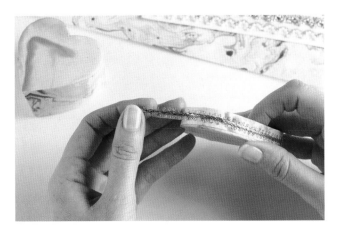

6 To complete the box, trim the edge of the lid with a strip of self-adhesive ribbon.

There's no reason why the papers covering the box base and lid should be the same, so why not mix and match plain and patterned papers to create a range of coordinating boxes? Here a deep red base sets off the delicate pink and white marbled lid, and a pearl and gold trim lends the box a vintage feel.

V A R I A T I O N

With love

Want to add some individuality to a wedding present? Then look no further! This design for a gift tag and matching paper lets you match your gift-wrapping to the shades chosen by the bride and groom for their big day. We also made the boxes on page 50 in the same colors to create a coordinated set of wedding gift-wrapping.

YOU WILL NEED

clear embossing ink	ruler
rubber stamp	8$^{1}/_{4}$ x 6 in. (21 x 15 cm) sheet of purple cardstock
8$^{1}/_{4}$ x 6 in. (21 x 15 cm) sheet of white paper	8$^{1}/_{4}$ x 6 in. (21 x 15 cm) sheet of sparkly purple cardstock
embossing heat gun	paper crimper/ribbler
craft chalks in purple, lilac, and pink	decorative-edge scissors
cotton balls	double-sided tape
pencil	

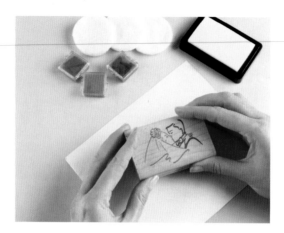

1 Ink the rubber stamp with the clear embossing ink then stamp the image onto the piece of white paper.

2 With the embossing heat gun, set the ink to ensure the image does not smudge during the next step.

3 Pick up a little chalk on a cotton ball and rub it over the image using a smooth circular motion. Repeat the process with the second and third shades of chalk.

4 With the pencil, lightly mark out a rectangle around the chalked image then use the ruler to tear the paper down to size.

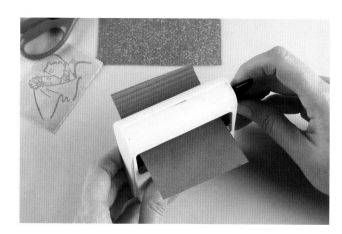

5 Cut a piece of the purple cardstock slightly larger than the stamped image. Make the sparkly purple cardstock slightly larger again. Run the first piece of cardstock through the paper crimper/ribbler.

TIP

- To prevent the chalk from coming off the paper, spray it lightly with a little hair spray to seal the chalk to the surface.

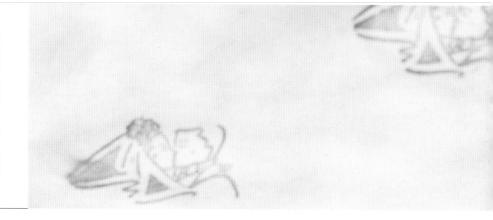

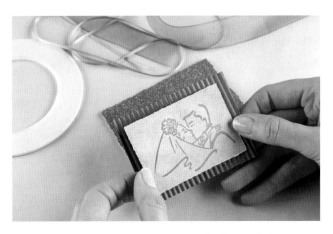

6 Take the sparkly piece of card and decorate the edges by cutting them with the decorative-edge scissors.

7 Using the double-sided tape, attach the chalked image to the center of the ribbled card.

8 Use a strip of double-sided tape down the left-hand side of the decorated card to attach it to the base card. Write your message on a slip of white paper and fix this between the two layers. If you wish, decorate the tag with a strip of knotted ribbon.

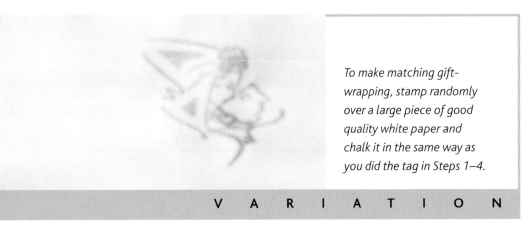

To make matching gift-wrapping, stamp randomly over a large piece of good quality white paper and chalk it in the same way as you did the tag in Steps 1–4.

V A R I A T I O N

Wedding gift boxes

These great little boxes are ideal either for presenting small wedding gifts, holding confetti, or as favors on the wedding tables. The template at the back of the book is designed so you can produce two boxes from one piece of cardstock measuring 16$\frac{1}{2}$ x 12 in. (42 x 30 cm).

YOU WILL NEED

template from page 139

craft knife

cutting mat

ruler

pencil

12 x 8 $\frac{1}{4}$ in. (30 x 21 cm) sheet of sparkly purple cardstock

embossing tool

8$\frac{1}{4}$ x 6 in. (21 x 15 cm) sheet of sparkly silver cardstock

decorative-edge punch

ribbon (narrow enough to fit the punched edge)

adhesive tape

double-sided tape

1 Photocopy the gift box template and transfer it to the back of the sheet of sparkly purple cardstock. Cut out the box shape, then score along the fold lines with the embossing tool.

TIP

• These boxes can also be used as place settings at a regular dinner: simply write your guests' names on them.

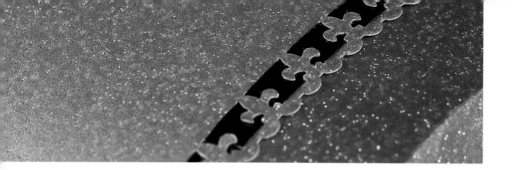

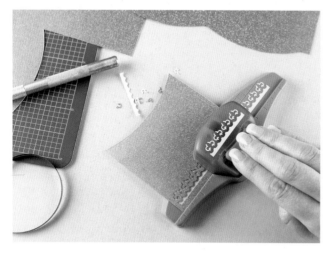

2 Transfer the template for the front section of the box to the sparkly silver card and cut it out. Punch along the long straight edge of the cardstock with the decorative-edge punch.

3 Thread the ribbon in and out of the punched design. For a neat finish, fold the ends of the ribbon around to the back of the cardstock and stick them down with adhesive tape.

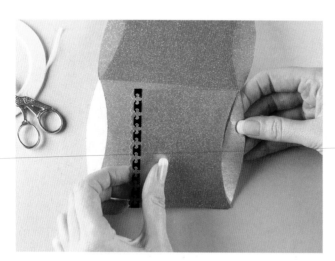

4 Fold along the scored lines on the box base then open them out again. Stick the trimmed piece of sparkly silver cardstock to the box, matching the curved edge with the folds you have just made on the box base.

5 To make up the box, run a piece of double-sided tape down one long edge, and fold the sides together. Using the creases made in Step 4, fold up the bottom of the box. Insert your gift, and close the top flaps to seal the box.

Turn leftover scraps of cardstock into matching tags for your wedding gifts. Use the decorative-edge punch and thread through a length of ribbon using the technique described in Steps 2 and 3, opposite.

V A R I A T I O N

Happy Halloween

To thank guests for coming and making your Halloween party such a success, why not give them a "Thank you" gift hidden within fun gift bags, themed for the occasion? The idea can be adapted to suit any number of events, for adults and children. For a slightly different method of making party bags, turn to Pretty in Pink on page 58.

YOU WILL NEED

template from page 140

12 x 8¼ in. (30 x 21 cm) sheet of marbled paper

scissors

rubber stamp

black ink pad

embossing tool

pencil

ruler

hole punch

double-sided tape

ribbon

1 Copy the template onto the wrong side of the marbled paper, then cut it out. To make folding the tabs easier, cut small slivers of paper either side of the cut lines on the tabs.

2 Turn the paper over and randomly stamp over the marbled surface with your chosen design. Leave the ink to dry.

3 On the wrong side of the paper, score along the fold lines using the embossing tool. Fold the bag into shape, then unfold again.

4 Fold down the top tabs, then make a pencil mark ¹/₂ in. (12 mm) down and 1 in. (2.5 cm) in from each side of the top edge as marked on the template. Punch four holes for the ribbon where you have made the marks.

5 Turn the paper over to the right side and score the two side folds. marked with dashes and dots on the template.

6 Using double-sided tape, stick the side and base tabs in place to create the bag.

7 Thread the ribbon through the four holes made in Step 4 and tie off to complete the bag.

Change the shade of the marbled paper and the design of the stamp to create gift bags that match the theme of your party. Ensure no party favors escape by closing the top of the bag with a bow.

V A R I A T I O N

Pretty in pink

This gorgeous gift bag is quick and easy to make, and the little pocket on the side of the bag is perfect for holding a special message or a gift voucher. The bag is made with store-bought wrapping paper, but this is the ideal project to make with one of the decorated papers from pages 22–35. Choose a coordinating plain or patterned paper for the pocket, and finish off the bag with pieces of ribbon.

YOU WILL NEED

templates from page 141

16 1/2 x 12 in. (42 x 30 cm) sheet of patterned wrapping paper

3 1/2 x 2 1/2 in. (8.5 x 6.5 cm) sheet of matching plain paper

cutting mat

ruler

craft knife

embossing tool

double-sided tape

dry glue stick

hole punch

ribbon

1 Photocopy the template onto the patterned side of the wrapping paper then cut it out. Make sure that the long, horizontal base line is nearest to you. Score along all the lines with the embossing tool to give you neat folds.

2 Cut out the pocket shape and make a concertina fold along the two short edges.

3 Stick narrow strips of double-sided tape down both sides and along the bottom of the pocket.

4 Peel the backing off the strips of tape and stick the pocket (open end up!) centrally on the front of the bag about 1½ in. (4 cm) down from the top edge.

5 Turn the bag over and fold up the bottom along the horizontal base line. Flatten it out again and turn the paper back over to the right side.

6 Using the printed lines as a guide, fold in the sides of the bag.

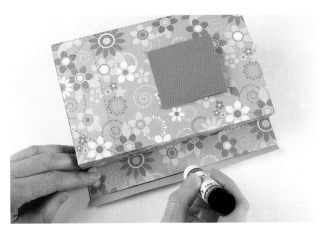

7 Fold up the side seam of the bag and stick it down with a line of adhesive.

8 Turn the bag upside down and make a base by folding in the sides. Fold over the flaps and fix them securely in position with double-sided tape. You may find it helps to place one hand in the bag as you press down.

9 Using a hole punch, make two holes in the same place on each side of the bag. Thread lengths of ribbon through the holes to make handles, then tape in place.

As an alternative to the main bag, why not make mini bags like the one shown here? They can be assembled in minutes, and make delightful and unusual place settings when filled with sugared almonds. Slip a card with each guest's name into the front pocket. Here, the pocket runs across the base of the bag, and the ribbon is threaded through the paper edge to make a decorative fastening. Mixing and matching plain and patterned papers adds to the interest.

V A R I A T I O N

Seasonal place settings

At Christmas time, you want the dinner table to be as special as the food you have prepared and with these elegant yet simple-to-make place settings it is bound to look festive. The method is so quick and easy you can make several place settings in no time at all. The quantities of cardstock given are enough for four places.

YOU WILL NEED

craft knife

cutting mat

pencil

ruler

12 x 8$\frac{1}{4}$ in. (30 x 21 cm) sheet of silver cardstock

embossing tool

12 x 8$\frac{1}{4}$ in. (30 x 21 cm) sheet of red cardstock

silver peel 'n' stick motifs

silver peel 'n' stick borders

double-sided tape

TIPS

• When working with small peel 'n' stick motifs, you may find it easier to pick them up with a fine pair of craft tweezers.

• If you have difficulty positioning peel 'n' sticks, remove the outside of the peel 'n' stick first, leaving just the motif on the backing paper. Then take a piece of low-tack adhesive tape and remove a little of the adhesive by first sticking it to your clothes or a piece of kitchen towel. Pick up the motif by placing the tape over it, transfer the motif to the card, then carefully remove the tape to leave the motif exactly where you want it.

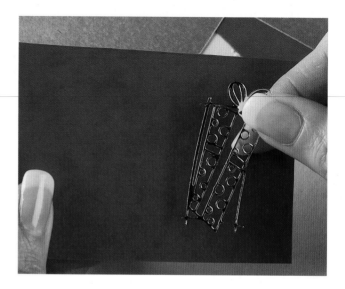

1 To make the base of the place setting, cut a rectangle of silver cardstock 4$\frac{1}{4}$ x 3 in. (11 x 8 cm) and score down the center with the embossing tool. Fold in half and set aside for use in Step 5. Cut a piece of red cardstock 4 x 2$\frac{3}{4}$ in. (10 x 7 cm) and stick a peel 'n' stick motif on the right-hand side.

2 Use the ruler to find the center of the card and score along the length either side of the motif. Make sure you do not score across the motif itself.

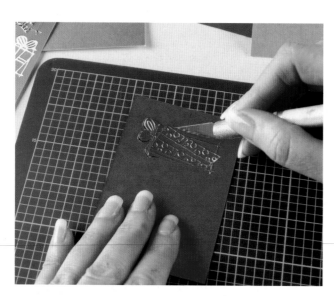

3 Using the craft knife, carefully cut around the part of the motif that is above the score line. Cut from one side of the motif to the other, starting at the score line and stopping when you reach the score line on the other side.

4 Fold the red cardstock along the score line so the motif sticks up. Outline the side and bottom edges with peel 'n' sticks borders.

5 To complete the place setting, attach the decorated card to the silver base made in Step 1 with strips of double-sided tape.

Mix and match peel 'n' stick motifs to create different versions of the place setting. Quick and easy to make, these cards are ideal for when you have hardly any time for crafting.

V A R I A T I O N

Shell place settings

A square of plain white cardstock folded in half makes the perfect base for these delightfully simple place cards. Any small shell can be used, so long as you choose a strong glue to fix them to the card base. The amount of cardstock here will be enough to make eight place cards.

YOU WILL NEED

craft knife

cutting mat

pencil

ruler

16^1/$_2$ x 12 in. (42 x 30 cm) sheet of white cardstock

embossing tool

non-water soluble craft glue

assorted shells

1 Using the pencil and ruler, draw a square 4 x 4 in. (10 cm) on the cardstock. Cut out the square with the craft knife.

2 Draw a faint line along the middle of the card, then score across it with the embossing tool. Fold the card in half then unfold it again.

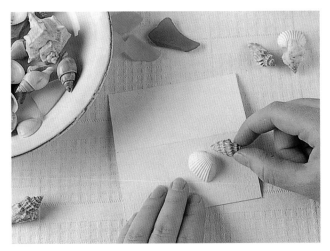

3 Spread glue over the inside edge of a shell and position it on the right-hand side of the card. Add more if you desire, then leave to dry overnight before writing the guest's name on the card.

CHAPTER **FOUR**

Greeting Cards and Invitations

Special occasions deserve truly original invitations and cards, and this chapter contains imaginative designs for weddings, anniversaries, birthdays, and more. From romantic scroll invitations to collage cards for kids, you'll find plenty of inspiration here.

Seductive scroll

This old-fashioned scroll design is so romantic that it makes a marvelously different invitation or birthday greeting. Best of all, it is very simple to make. The project uses four different weights of paper, including a handmade one. What could be more charming than a scroll made with paper you have crafted yourself?

YOU WILL NEED

pencil

ruler

craft knife

cutting mat

12 x 8 1/4 in. (30 x 21 cm) sheet of gold-flecked transparent paper

12 x 8 1/4 in. (30 x 21 cm) sheet of marbled paper

spray glue

12 x 8 1/4 in. (30 x 21 cm) sheet of handmade paper

12 x 8 1/4 in. (30 x 21 cm) sheet of tracing paper

4 eyelets

punch and eyelet setter

thin ribbon in matching shade

scissors

pen

thick ribbon in matching shade

1 Trim the transparent paper down to 11 x 7 1/2 in. (28 x 19 cm), and fix it to the center of the marbled paper with spray glue. Trim the handmade paper down to 10 x 6 3/4 in. (25.5 x 17 cm) and make the tracing paper about 1 in. (2.5 cm) smaller all around than this.

TIP

• If the transparent paper is creased, iron it on a low heat to remove the creases before you start crafting.

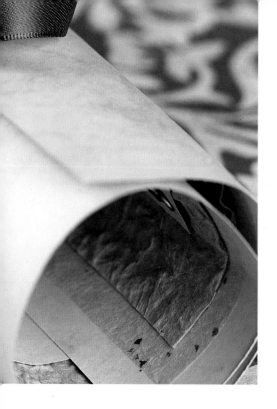

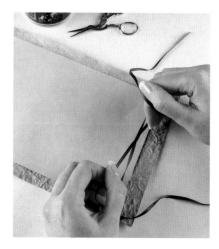

2 Using the punch and eyelet setter, attach the tracing paper to the center of the handmade paper by fixing an eyelet in each corner.

3 Thread the thin ribbon through the eyelets at the top of the paper and back through the eyelets at the bottom. Tie the ribbon in a small bow and trim off the ends.

4 With the spray glue, fix this pair of papers to the center of the pair you made in Step 1.

5 Write your message on the scroll, then gently roll it up and wrap it tightly with the thicker ribbon. Tie the ribbon in a bow to keep the scroll sealed.

TIP

- A scroll made from lightweight paper that won't spring open can be sealed with a dollop of sealing wax. Decorate the seal with any small patterned object, such as a coin or a ring.

To create an alternative look, try layering the papers on the outside of your scroll.

Special memories

Remind friends or relatives of their wedding day by picking a favorite photograph and turning it into a stunning 3-D anniversary card. This is an ideal project for making good use of your own sponged paper (see Sponging, page 32).

YOU WILL NEED

two 12 x 8 1/4 in. (30 x 21 cm) sheets of purple cardstock

ruler

8 1/4 x 6 in. (21 x 15 cm) sheet of sponged paper in matching colors

double-sided tape

small scissors

4 copies of a photograph

double-sided foam dots

ribbon flowers

matching ribbon

hot glue gun

1 Fold one sheet of purple cardstock in half to make the greeting card base. Using the ruler to ensure a straight edge, tear off about 1/2 in. (12 mm) from all four edges of the sponged paper to make it slightly smaller than the card base. Attach the sponged paper to the front of the greeting card with double-sided tape. (Place the sponged paper at a slight angle to give the card more "movement.") Set aside for use in Step 5.

2 With a small pair of scissors, carefully cut out one complete photograph. On the second card, cut out the bride and groom, but this time remove the background. On the third card, remove slightly more of the image, leaving elements that appear to be at the front of the scene. On the last card, just leave those elements that really stand out, such as the bouquet in our example.

3 Tear a piece from the second sheet of purple cardstock, making it about 1 in. (2.5 cm) larger than the first photograph. Fix the photograph to the cardstock with double-sided tape. Mount the second photograph on top of the first using double-sided tape around the sides and bottom, and double-sided foam dots in the middle.

TIPS

- To create four identical images, either print them off from your home computer, photocopy them, or get multiple copies made at a photo store.

- If running off the photograph from your home computer, you can add a little nostalgia to the image by removing the color and making a softly toned sepia or black and white photograph, as shown here.

4 Add the third then the fourth photographs from Step 2, using double-sided foam dots between them to create a 3-D effect.

5 Mount the completed 3-D image at a slight angle on the left-hand side of the greeting card with double-sided foam dots. To complete the greeting card, tie a bow around the flowers then fix them to the base using the hot glue gun.

"Thank you!"

Sometimes choosing just the right card to say "Thank you" to a friend seems almost impossible. So why not make a card with a bunch of flowers on the front to convey the message for you?

YOU WILL NEED

flower hobby punch

8¼ x 6 in. (21 x 15 cm) sheet of marbled paper

7 self-adhesive flat backed diamond jewels

16½ x 12 in. (42 x 30 cm) sheet of green cardstock

craft knife

cutting mat

pencil

ruler

card-folding board (optional)

bone folder

8¼ x 6 in. (21 x 15 cm) sheet of turquoise handmade paper

double-sided tape

7 x 5 in. (18 x 13 cm) sheet of transparent handmade paper

double-sided foam tape

double-sided foam dots

wire cutters

green wire

ribbon

1 Punch seven flowers with the hobby punch from the marbled paper. Peel off the backing and stick a diamond jewel to the center of each flower.

2 Cut the sheet of green cardstock in half and make two folds about 3 in. (7 cm) in from the short sides with the bone folder to create a gatefold card. (Set aside the second half of cardstock for use in Step 4.)

3 Fold both flaps into the center to make the card base. Attach the turquoise handmade paper to the left-hand flap of the base card with strips of double-sided tape.

4 Cut a piece 4 x 6 in. (10 x 15 cm) from the leftover piece of cardstock from Step 2. Lay the cardstock in the center of the transparent handmade paper, then wrap the edges around the cardstock and fix it in place with strips of double-sided tape.

5 Mount the covered card centrally on the front of the greeting card base with pieces of double-sided foam tape.

6 Cut seven pieces of wire approximately 4 in. (10 cm) long and stick them in place on the front of the card with double-sided foam dots. Curve the wires slightly so they look like flower stems.

TIPS

• If you can't get hold of thick handmade paper use thin handmade paper mounted on a piece of the base cardstock instead.

• If you don't have a card-folding board such as the one used in Step 2, use an embossing tool or a ball point pen that no longer works to score the card.

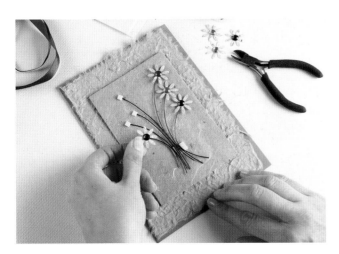

7 At the top of each wire "stem," attach a flower head with more double-sided foam dots.

8 Tie the ribbon into a bow and stick it to the point where the wire stems cross with more double-sided foam dots.

If you punch out the flowers evenly along the piece of marbled paper in Step 1, you can use the "waste" to create a completely different card. In this way, you get two unique cards for the price of one!

V A R I A T I O N

Animal magic

Finding the perfect greeting card for a youngster can sometimes be a chore, so try making them a fun card using one of our animal face templates. Better still, encourage children to make their own animal cards for friends. Let them do the collage, but help them fix the eyelets.

YOU WILL NEED

templates from pages 142–45

12 x 8 1/4 in. (30 x 21 cm) sheet of white paper

scissors

pencil

12 x 8 1/4 in. (30 x 21 cm) sheet of bronze cardstock

8 1/4 x 6 in. (21 x 15 cm) sheet of green paper

assorted 12 x 8 1/4 in. (30 x 21 cm) sheets of paper in different shades to suit the animal face chosen

dry glue stick

4 eyelets

punch and eyelet setter

fluffy decorative thread

black marker pen

silver pen

1 Copy the template of your desired animal onto a sheet of white paper and cut out each element of the design separately: the face shape, the ears, the nose, and so on.

TIP

• As you work, keep a copy of the template of your chosen animal on the desk so you can follow it as you build up the face.

2 With a pencil, trace around each of these elements on a shade of paper that suits the part of the animal's face, then carefully tear out the shape.

3 Fold the bronze cardstock in half to make the base of the greeting card. Tear off about 1/2 in. (12 mm) from around the piece of green paper and then attach it to the front of the greeting card with the dry glue stick. Fix an eyelet in each corner.

4 Thread the fluffy decorative thread through the eyelets and tie it off at the back. Use the dry glue stick to fix the pieces of the animal's face to the front of the card.

5 When you have glued all the paper pieces in position, complete the design by drawing in the features the black marker pen. Add highlights, such as the shine on the lion's nose, with the silver pen.

TIP

- You can add depth to the design by sticking some of the elements in place with double-sided foam dots.

Jazz up a store-bought, brown-paper bag with a matching animal face for a quick and easy solution to your gift-wrapping dilemma.

V A R I A T I O N

Celebration time

From the outside this may look like an ordinary greeting card but—when opened—it springs a little surprise on you! A simple pop-up mechanism adds punch to the design, and the rich colors make this stylish card suitable for birthdays or special holiday celebrations, such as Christmas or Hanukah.

In this project, you can use your own handmade spattered paper (see Spattering, page 34). To make the stencil for embossing the candle motif see Making a stencil on page 26.

YOU WILL NEED

craft knife	red decorative thread
cutting mat	ruler
two 12 x 8 1/4 in. (30 x 21 cm) sheets of red cardstock	double-sided foam dots
decorative-edge scissors	FOR THE STENCIL
12 x 8 1/4 in. (30 x 21 cm) sheet of spattered cream paper	template from page 146
	thin cardstock
8 1/4 x 6 in. (21 x 15 cm) sheet of gold cardstock	pencil
	embossing tool
double-sided tape	light box

1   Cut one sheet of red cardstock in half so you have two rectangles, each 8$\frac{1}{4}$ x 6 in. (21 x 15 cm). Fold one rectangle in half to make the base of the greeting card. (Keep the second rectangle for use in Step 6.) With the decorative-edge scissors, cut out a piece of spattered card 5 x 4 in. (13 x 10 cm).

2   Mount the trimmed spattered paper centrally on the greeting card base with double-sided tape. With the decorative-edge scissors, cut a rectangle of red cardstock 3$\frac{3}{4}$ x 3$\frac{1}{4}$ in. (9.5 x 8.5 cm). Wrap the thread around the rectangle of card, fixing it in place on the reverse with double-sided foam dots.

3   Mount the wrapped piece of red cardstock on the center of the greeting card base using double-sided foam dots.

4   With the decorative-edge scissors, cut out a piece of gold cardstock 2$\frac{3}{4}$ x 2$\frac{1}{2}$ in. (7 x 6.5 cm) and pressure-emboss the candle design following the instructions on page 29. Make a second embossed card for use in Step 8.

5 Mount one embossed card centrally on the front of the greeting card with double-sided foam dots. (Note that this is a horizontal card.)

6 Now make the pop-up part of the greeting card. Take the second piece of red cardstock from Step 1 and trim about 1/8 in. (3 mm) from one short side and one long side before folding it in half. Working on the folded edge, measure in 2 1/4 in. (6 cm) from both sides and make a cut in the card at right angles to the fold about 1/2 in. (12 mm) long.

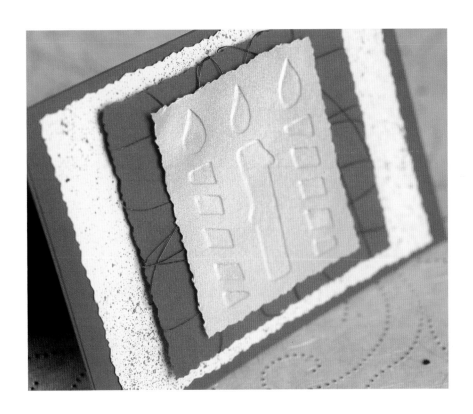

7 On the outside of the card, score a line between the cuts on each side of the central fold with the embossing tool. Push this piece inside the card to create a small step.

8 With the decorative-edge scissors, cut a piece of spattered paper 7$\frac{1}{2}$ x 5$\frac{1}{2}$ in. (19 x 14 cm) to fit in the card. Cut out a small section so the paper sits around the step you have just created. Fix in place with double-sided tape. Take the second piece of embossed gold card from Step 4 and stick it to the step with more tape: when the card is opened the gold card will stand up, as shown below.

9 Use double-sided tape to fix the pop-up insert inside the decorated outer card to complete the greeting card.

Why not re-use the candle stencil to make matching wrapping paper? Rub a little red and orange craft chalk over a sheet of plain white paper, then push more chalk through the stencil with a sponge. See Using a stencil to add color on page 28, but use chalk instead of ink.

VARIATION

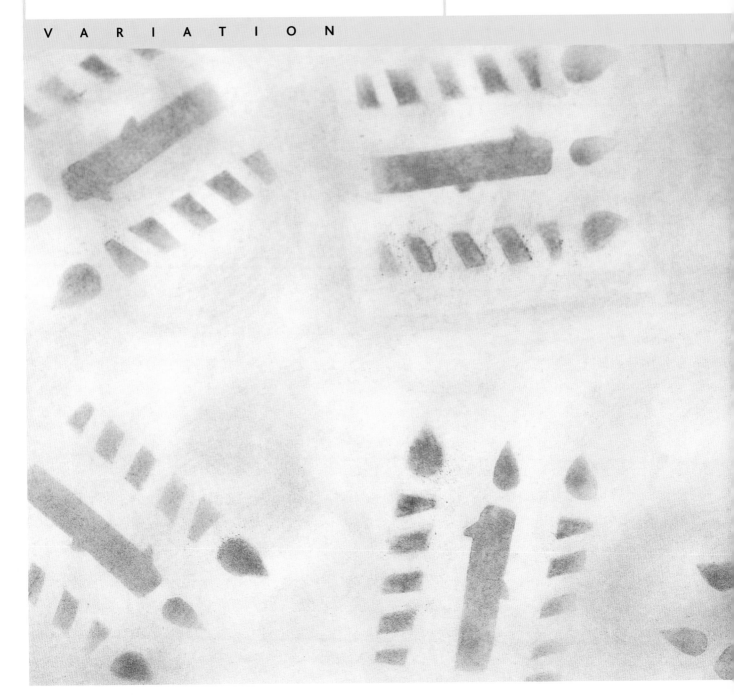

Be my Valentine

Use a little wire-and-bead magic to show someone how much you care with this stylish but simple Valentine's card. Here we used seed beads and red wire, but tiny crystals on fine silver wire would be equally eye-catching.

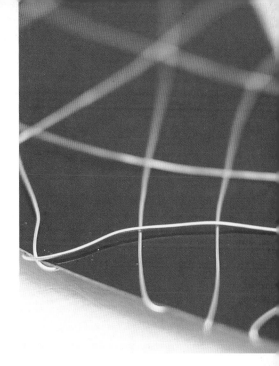

YOU WILL NEED

bone folder

card-folding board (optional)

8¼ x 6 in. (21 x 15 cm) sheet of handmade rose petal paper

12 x 8¼ in. (30 x 21 cm) sheet of red cardstock

double-sided tape

wire cutters

22 gauge silver or red wire

pencil

scissors

approx. 200 seed beads

template from page 148

double-sided foam dots

adhesive tape

TIP

- If you need to tear a piece of handmade paper down to size, first "draw" along the tear line with a damp brush. Tear along the damp line using a ruler to ensure a straight line.

1 Score down the center of the handmade petal paper and fold it in half. Cut the red cardstock in half, and score one half down the middle and fold to make the greeting card base. Set aside the other half for use in Step 4.

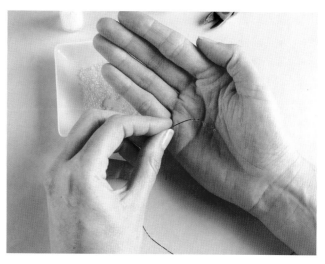

2 Place double-sided tape along the back folded edge of the red greeting card base and wrap the handmade paper around it, pressing along the fold to ensure the paper sticks to the tape.

3 Cut 2 feet (60 cm) of wire, then thread on enough seed beads to cover about 2 in. (5 cm) of the wire.

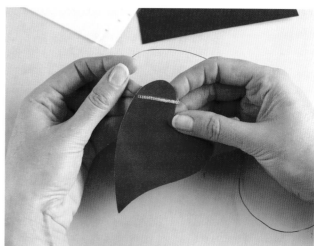

4 Transfer the template to the second piece of red cardstock from Step 1 and cut it out. Use a double-sided foam dots to fix one end of the beaded wire to the top of the heart (on the wrong side) and bring the wire to the front of the heart. Make sure all the beads come to the front.

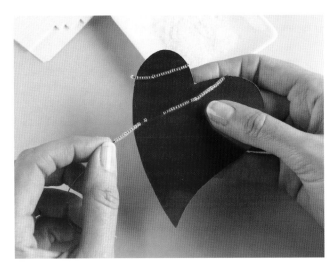

5 Continue to add beads and to wind the wire until the heart has five strands of beading wrapped around it, all fixed to the back with double-sided foam dots. When you have finished adding the beads and winding, fix the end of the wire to the wrong side of the heart with adhesive tape.

6 Mount the heart centrally to the front of the greeting card using double-sided foam dots.

For a simple but striking alternative, use silver wire wrapped several times around a heart shape. Even without beads, a silver and red Valentine's card looks stunning.

V A R I A T I O N

Party!

If you are looking for an invitation that is a little different, why not have a go at this pretty design? The invitation uses easy-to-create balloon-punched shapes that are then embellished with the decorative touch of a silver pen. If you print out the text of your invitation on a computer, you can make lots of these invitations quite quickly.

YOU WILL NEED

8¹/₄ x 6 in. (21 x 15 cm) sheet of green cardstock
four 8¹/₄ x 6 in. (21 x 15 cm) sheets of cardstock in matching shades
pencil
ruler
craft knife
cutting mat
12 x 8¹/₄ in. (30 x 21 cm) sheet of tracing paper
double-sided tape
8¹/₄ x 6 in. (21 x 15 cm) sheet of turquoise handmade paper
balloon hobby punch
sticky paper strips
silver pen
double-sided foam dots
wired ribbon
clear-drying craft glue

1 To make the inner part of the invitation, fold the piece of green cardstock in half then open it out again. With the pencil and ruler, mark out an aperture on one side of the card making sure you leave a border at least ¹/₂ in. (12 mm) wide. Carefully cut out the aperture.

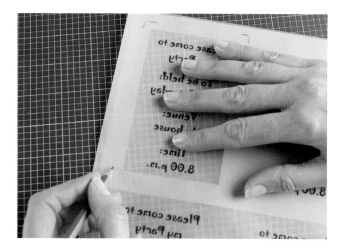

2 Print out the text of your invitation on tracing paper, first checking that the words will fit inside the aperture. Place the tracing paper over the aperture and mark out where you need to cut, ensuring you leave a wide enough paper border to stick it in place.

3 Cut out the text and fix it in place with strips of double-sided tape. Make sure the wrong side of the text faces you so when you turn the card back over it reads in the right direction. Apply strips of double-sided tape around the tracing paper, then fold the front and back of the card together to seal the text inside.

4 Fold the handmade paper in half. Place double-sided tape down the back fold on the inner card and wrap the handmade paper around it to fix it in place.

5 Punch out some balloon shapes in the four shades of cardstock. Wrap a tiny piece of sticky paper strip at the neck of each balloon, then add a highlight with the silver pen.

6 Create ties for the balloons with sticky paper strips, crossing them over at the bottom as if they were all tied together.

7 Use dots of clear-drying craft glue to stick some of the balloons directly onto the handmade paper at the top end of the ties. Fix others in place with the double-sided foam dots so they are slightly raised from the surface.

8 Tie a bow in the wired ribbon and cut the ends at an angle. Shape the bow then stick it in place with the clear-drying craft glue.

If you are short of time, cut out an aperture in a small piece of handmade paper, back it with a matching shade of card, and sandwich the invitation details between the two pieces. Decorate the frame with a few punched balloons and you will have an even quicker version of the invitation!

V A R I A T I O N

CHAPTER **FIVE**

Manipulating Paper

In chapter five you will find ideas for both flat and 3-D decoupage, designs for handmade folders, inspiration for personalizing frames, and much more. From a woven basket and book cover, to themed bunting, you'll discover plenty of ways to transform sheets of paper into fabulous objects.

Floral box

With decoupage, you can personalize all kinds of surfaces in barely any time at all. Store-bought boxes are not only great for storing all your knick-knacks, but they also make perfect bases for decoupage. This small box makes a handy container for earrings and other small jewelry items.

YOU WILL NEED

household paint or water-based craft paint

small household paintbrush

store-bought cardboard box

flower and leaf paper punches

two 8 $\frac{1}{4}$ x 6 in. (21 x 15 cm) sheets of paper in medium and dark blue

non-toxic water-soluble craft glue

small pot to hold water

self-adhesive ribbon

TIPS

• Tester pots of household paint are great for painting small objects. They are cheap and available in a wide range of shades, which makes them very economical for this type of project. Alternatively, craft paints work just as well.

1 Remove any labels then paint the box base and lid and let dry. Give the box a second coat of paint if required.

2 Using the flower and leaf punches, punch out a selection of shapes from the two sheets of paper.

3 Make a mixture of craft glue and water (ratio 50:50). Use the paintbrush to coat the box base with this mixture, then scatter the leaf and flower shapes on the sticky surface of the box in a random fashion.

4 When you have covered the box base with leaves and flowers, coat each of the shapes with a layer of the craft glue and water mixture. Repeat Steps 3 and 4 to decorate the box lid, but do not stick any shapes along the lip. Allow the top and bottom pieces to dry, then give the box a second coat of craft glue and water to seal the surface and make it hardwearing.

5 To complete the project, wrap a strip of ribbon around
  the lip of the lid.

Teddy box

Stamping lends itself brilliantly to 3-D decoupage, so get stamping and create this cute box, which is ideal for a baby's first gift. You'll find plenty more hints and tips on different methods of stamping on pages 24–25.

YOU WILL NEED

rubber stamp

black pigment ink

12 x 8¼ in. (30 x 21 cm) cream cardstock or thick paper

clear embossing powder

embossing heat gun

water-soluble pencils

waterbrush or a fine artists' paintbrush and a small pot to hold water

small scissors

10¼ x 9¾ in. (26 x 25 cm) sheet of dark red cardstock, trimmed down fraction all around(box base)

10¼ x 9¾ in. (26 x 25 cm) sheet of dark red cardstock (box top)

bone folder

5½ x 5⅛ in. (14 x 13 cm) sheet of dark orange cardstock

4¾ x 4¼ in. (12 x 11 cm) sheet of spattered cream cardstock

4 x 3½ in. (10 x 9 cm) sheet of light orange cardstock

double-sided tape

double-sided foam dots

1 Stamp the image four times on the cream cardstock then emboss the images with clear embossing powder. Use the embossing heat gun to melt the powder then let cool.

2 Color in the four images with the water-soluble pencils, creating a watercolor effect with a waterbrush or a paintbrush dipped in water.

3 Cut out the first image, including the background. Cut out the second image, but remove the background. Remove all of the background and some of the figure from the third image. Remove even more of the figure from the final piece. Set all four layers to one side for use in Step 6.

4 To make the box, use the bone folder to score 1 1/2 in. (4 cm) in along all four edges on both pieces of dark red cardstock.

TIPS

- If you have a multicolored stamp pad, you can use this to render the stamped image. Dampen a paintbrush, pick up a little color from the pad, and use it in the same way as watercolor.

- To save time, color in only those parts of the stamp that will show once the figures have been cut out (here, the teddy and bunny).

- Write "base" lightly with a pencil on the smaller piece of dark red cardstock so you can easily identify it later.

5 To make the flaps for the box base, cut in from the outer edges to the score lines, one cut along each side. (Cutting tiny slivers of paper either side of the cut lines will make folding the flaps easier.) Repeat to make the box lid.

6 Take the box lid (that is, the larger piece of dark red cardstock) and mount the dark orange cardstock, the spattered cardstock, and the light orange cardstock in the top right-hand corner (inside the score lines) with double-sided tape. Mount the four layers of the image one on top of the other with double-sided foam dots to create a 3-D effect.

7 Place some double-sided tape on each flap of the box lid and fold in the sides. Complete the box base in the same way.

TIP

- For that finishing touch add a piece of ribbon or a bow to the completed box.

Fancy frame

If you are finding it difficult to locate just the right frame for an unusual photograph, try making and decorating your own frame with brightly colored crepe paper and a matching thread. By changing the colors, this frame will fit into any room scheme. Our frame takes photographs 6 x 4¹⁄₄ in. (15 x 11 cm). If your photograph is a different size then you will have to alter the sizes of the aperture and inner edges of the spacer.

YOU WILL NEED

templates from page 149

craft knife

cutting mat

pencil

ruler

16¹⁄₂ x 12 in. (42 x 30 cm) sheet of thick cardstock

craft glue

1 roll of green crepe paper

scissors

double-sided tape

decorative green thread

adhesive tape

1 Using the templates from the back of the book, cut out all four sections of the frame from the thick cardstock. Stick the spacer to the back piece of the frame with a thin line of craft glue.

NOTE In Step 1, do not apply glue between the spacer arms when fixing the spacer to the back piece: this is where the photograph is slipped into the frame.

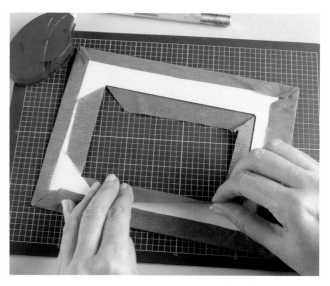

2 Place the back piece with the spacer attached on the crepe paper. Cut out the crepe paper with the scissors, leaving a 1/2-in. (12-mm) overlap around the back piece. Stick the crepe paper to the spacer with strips of double-sided tape, gently folding it down to give a neat finish.

3 Cover the front section of the frame in the same way as you did the back in Step 2. However, to create a neat finish to the aperture, cut into the crepe paper at the corners using the craft knife, then fold it back and fix it to the wrong side of the card with strips of double-sided tape.

4 Tear the crepe paper into several strips, each about 1/2 or 3/4 in. (12 mm or 2 cm) wide. Attach one end of the crepe paper to the back of the aperture with double-sided tape and begin to wind it around the frame. Continue until you have covered the frame completely, neatening the ends with the scissors. Fix the last strip of crepe paper in position at the back of the frame with more tape.

5 Wind the decorative string around the aperture of the frame until you are happy with the effect, then attach the end to the back of the aperture with adhesive tape.

6 Apply thin lines of craft glue to the bottom and side edges of the frame, and fix the decorated front section to the back, sandwiching the spacer between the front and back sections. (The photograph will be slipped into the frame between the spacer arms.) Place the frame under some heavy books for a couple of hours until the glue has dried. Score down the long side of the the stand as shown in the photograph (left) and fold it in to 90 degrees. Fix the stand to the back of the frame with plenty of adhesive tape, making sure the bottom edges of the frame and stand are even.

V A R I A T I O N

Use our smaller template to create mini frames that make adorable gifts and unusual Christmas tree decorations!

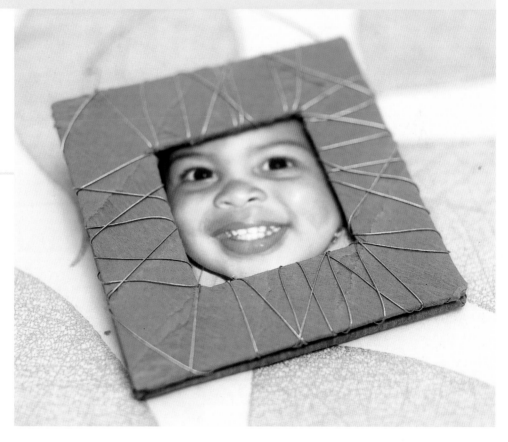

Stationery folder

Looking for a gift that the avid letter writer would love? Then why not try out this stationery folder? The body of the folder is made from a thick cardstock that is covered in handmade paper then embellished with beads. Personalizing the folder with a special photograph is guaranteed to appeal to the recipient and make it truly memorable.

YOU WILL NEED

template from page 151
craft knife
cutting mat
pencil
ruler
23^1/$_2$ x 16^1/$_2$ in. (59.5 x 42 cm) sheet of thick cardstock
embossing tool
23^1/$_2$ x 16^1/$_2$ in. (59.5 x 42 cm) sheet of handmade paper
scissors
approx. 150 seed beads
sewing thread
short beading needle
double-sided tape
1^1/$_2$ (40 cm) ribbon

TIP

- Some double-sided tapes do not adhere well to handmade papers. Before you begin, do a test to make sure the brand of tape you are using works well with your paper. If it doesn't adhere well, choose a different brand.

1 Using the template, cut out the folder base from the thick cardstock and score along the fold lines with an embossing tool. Place the cardstock base on the handmade paper and trace around it. With the scissors, cut out the handmade paper slightly larger than the card and mark the fold lines on it with the pencil.

2 Remove the cardstock base from the handmade paper and use the pencil and ruler to draw in the two fold lines on the reverse of the paper.

3 On front section only, randomly sew the seed beads in place.

4 Stick the handmade paper to the cardstock base with strips of double-sided tape, wrapping the outside edges and the edges of the aperture over to create a neat finish.

5 Cut a piece of handmade paper slightly smaller than the back section of the folder and fix it in position with double-sided tape to give a neat finish to what will be the inside of the folder.

6 Cut two lengths of ribbon to about 8 in. (20 cm) and attach one to the inside of the inner flap. Place some double-sided tape down both sides, bring the flap up, and fix it in place.

7 In the other fold line, cut a hole level with the first piece of ribbon and thread the second piece of ribbon through to the right side, fixing the end in place with adhesive tape.

8 Fix the photograph in the aperture using double-sided tape.

9 Fold the back section over the back of the picture and seal in it place with more double-sided tape. Fill the folder with scented paper and slip in a pen to complete your gift.

Change the aperture shape and use a handmade paper with embedded leaves for a completely different look.

V A R I A T I O N

Paper-weave basket

This woven basket makes an unusual container in which to keep all kinds of lightweight items, from scented potpourri to delicious candy and chocolates. The weaving is quite tricky to begin with, but the basket gets easier to handle after the first upright strip has been positioned in Step 6.

YOU WILL NEED

craft knife

cutting mat

ruler

pencil

18 x 11 in. (45.5 x 28 cm) sheet of green paper

scrap paper to cover the work surface when adding gold pen highlights

gold pen

craft glue (in a bottle with a fine nozzle)

scissors

1 With the craft knife, cut the handmade paper into fourteen strips: ten strips each measuring $3/4$ in. (2 cm) wide and 12 in. (30 cm) long, and four strips each measuring $3/4$ in. (2 cm) wide and 18 in. (45.5 cm) long. Protecting the work surface with scrap paper, highlight the long edges of all the strips with the gold pen.

TIP

• If you do not have a craft glue bottle with a fine nozzle, use store-bought glue dots instead to hold the paper in place as you weave.

2 Take two of the 12-in. (30-cm) long strips and find the middle. Dab a blob of glue on the reverse of one strip and stick the two pieces together, face up, to make a cross.

3 Take two more 12-in. (30-cm) long strips and place these either side of the first vertical strip, under the horizontal strip. Hold both pieces in place with a dab of glue. Take another two strips and place them either side of the last two strips. However, this time place them over the horizontal strip (as shown in the photograph), again holding them in place with a dab of glue.

4 Work the remaining four 12-in. (30-cm) strips horizontally in the same way, weaving one under and one over as you work, and fixing them all in place with dabs of glue. This will be the base of your basket.

5 Turn the base over and fold the loose ends of each strip along the completed woven base. Take one of the 18-in. (45.5-cm) strips and weave it in and out at the bottom of the folded ends so the sides of the basket begin to form.

6 As you work, dab a blob of glue on the underside of the long strip and hold it with your fingertips for a moment so the glue dries. When you have worked around all four sides, cut off any excess paper with the scissors, and glue the ends in position.

7 Take a second 18-cm (45.5-cm) strip and weave it in and out around the sides, making sure that each weave is opposite to the one beneath. Repeat with the last two remaining strips until the basket is completed.

TIP

• Trim or fold in the top of the vertical strips or leave them loose as shown here, depending on the kind of finish you want.

8 Check over the basket to ensure everything is secure and, if any of the strips are loose, place a blob of glue underneath them and pinch together while the glue dries.

Chinese lantern

Jelly jars wrapped in pretty paper make great lanterns to decorate a dinner table, especially if the meal is held outdoors on a summer evening. Drop a tea light into the jar and light with a taper.

YOU WILL NEED

jelly jar

tape measure

12 x 8 1/4 in. (30 x 21 cm) sheet of thin, handmade paper

craft knife

cutting mat

pencil

ruler

double-sided tape

self-adhesive ribbon

1 To work out the size of paper you need, follow the instructions in the box (*right*). Cut out a piece of handmade paper to the required size and draw in the cutting and folding lines.

TO DRAW THE GRID LINES

1. Measure the height and circumference of the jelly jar and add 2 in. (5 cm) to the height and 3/8 in. (1 cm) to the circumference.

2. Draw a line the length of the paper, 3/8 in. (1 cm) in from the edge. This line is based on the circumference and becomes the base of the lantern.

2. Working from this line, draw a second line that measures the height of the jelly jar plus 3/4 in. (2 cm).

3. Measure 3/4 in. (2 cm) down from the second line and draw a line the length of the paper. This will be where the paper is attached to the top of the jelly jar.

4. Draw lines from the top of the paper to the bottom 3/8 in. (1 cm) apart, starting 3/4 in. (2 cm) in from the edge.

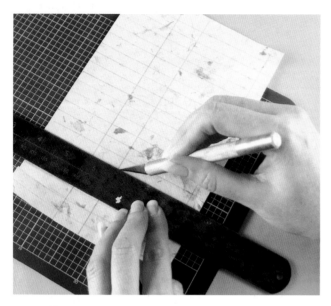

2 Following the grid lines, cut down the paper from the top edge to the third horizontal line drawn. Do not cut between the third and second horizontal lines. Then, cut between the second and the first line. Continue in this way, cutting the full length of the paper.

3 Place double-sided tape on the two sections that you have not cut—the center and the bottom edge—and wrap the paper around the jelly jar so that the tape sticks to the top and bottom of the jar.

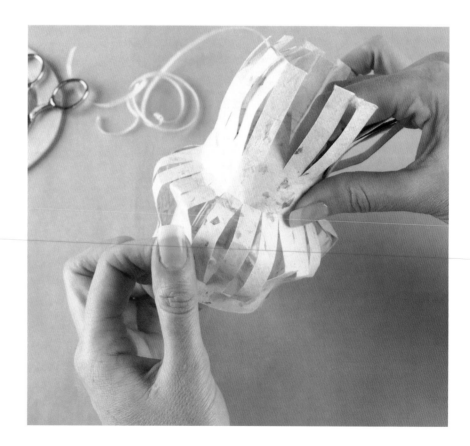

4 As you stick the paper to the jar, the cut sections should fan out. Gently ease out any that pop in.

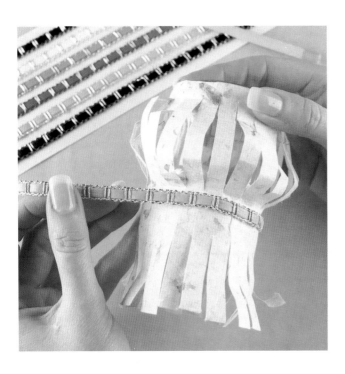

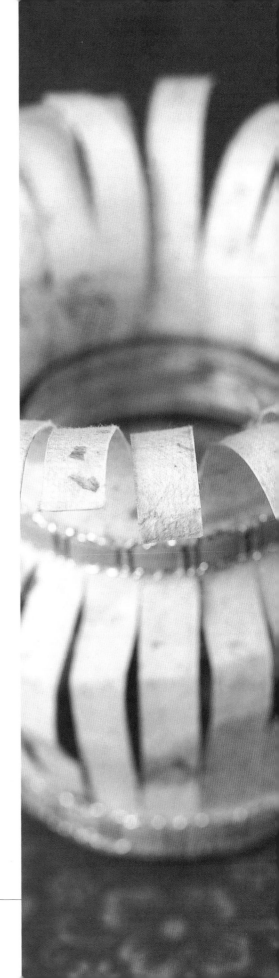

5   Wrap a piece of self-adhesive ribbon around the lantern at the top of the jar, cutting off any excess.

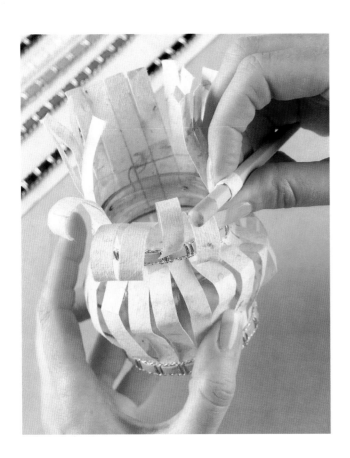

6   Use the pencil to curl the top of the paper away from the jar to complete the lantern.

Silhouette

Turn the photograph of a friend or family member into a classic silhouette, then use the shape to create a wonderfully different greeting card, place it in a frame to make an unusual gift, or hang it on a wall with a piece of ribbon. Remember to choose a photograph that shows the person in perfect profile.

YOU WILL NEED

small scissors

photograph

dry glue stick

$8^{1}/_{4}$ x 6 in. (21 x 15 cm) sheet of black paper

black marker pen

two $8^{1}/_{4}$ x 6 in. (21 x 15 cm) sheets of cardstock in matching shades

silver peel 'n' stick borders

1 Roughly cut around the photograph removing most of the background.

2 Stick the cut-out image onto the piece of black paper with the dry glue stick, then carefully cut around the facial features, removing all the unwanted areas.

3 Run the black marker pen around the edge of the image to remove any unsightly white sections that may be visible.

4 Turn the face over so the black paper is uppermost and mount it as desired with the dry glue stick. In our sample, we used two shades of card and trimmed it with silver peel 'n' stick borders.

Papercut bunting

When you are holding a party one of the many things on your list has to be decorations for the room. By making your own bunting, you can theme it to suit the celebration. Here we show you how to create some bunting for a Halloween party, and the variations provided as templates suggest designs for other occasions.

YOU WILL NEED

template from page 152

1 roll orange crepe paper

black marker pen

scissors

1 Place the template on the end of the crepe paper roll and draw around the pumpkin shape with the black marker pen, making sure both sides of the template touch the folded sections of the crepe paper.

2 With the scissors, carefully cut through all the layers around the shape you have drawn, making sure you leave enough paper at both sides to ensure the bunting does not fall apart.

TIPS

- Before you trace around the template ensure the width is the same as the folds of the crepe paper. If it is not, either scale the template up or down, or refold the paper.

- To make it easier to add the features in Step 3, place the template on a light box then place one section of bunting at a time over the template and trace through the features.

- When drawing anything on crepe paper, it is best to use short straight lines.

3 Unfold the bunting and add the details on the pumpkin's face with the black marker pen. Repeat Steps 1–3 on the next section of crepe paper to make further lengths of bunting, if you need them.

Other decorative features can be added to bunting in the form of glitter glue.

VARIATION

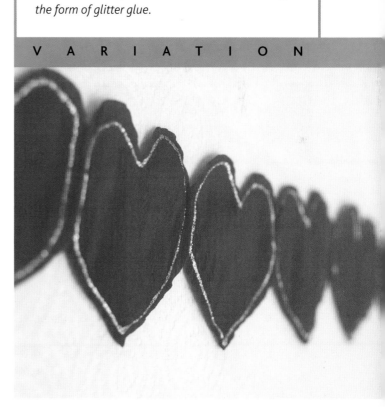

Cover up

An ordinary sketch book can be turned into something special with a little weaving magic. You may decide to limit your choice of colors, as we have here, or go for a wide range of hues for a multicolored effect.

YOU WILL NEED

craft knife

ruler

cutting mat

pencil

12 x 8 1/4 in. (30 x 21 cm) sheet cardstock to cover the book

assorted 12 x 8 1/4 in. (30 x 21 cm) sheets of paper and cardstock in matching shades

book to decorate

double-sided tape

1 Cut a piece of cardstock the same size as the front cover of your chosen book and set it aside for use in Step 2. Cut strips of paper and card in differing widths between 1/2 in. (12 mm) and 1 in. (2.5 cm), but make them all approximately 3/4 in. (2 cm) longer than the depth of the book.

2 Place a piece of double-sided tape along three edges of the base card: one along the top and one down either side. Attach strips running down the length of the card base, leaving an overhang of about $1/2$ in. (12 mm) at both ends of the strips.

V A R I A T I O N

Experiment with the way you weave the paper to create difference effects, for example one over, two under or under two, over two.

TIP

• If you find the paper strips move around while you are working, place a dab of glue underneath each strip to hold it in place as you weave.

3 When the base card is covered in horizontal strips, weave the first cross strip of paper or cardstock one over, one under from one side to the other. Make sure you leave an overhang at each end and that each strip is in straight. (Peel back some of the backing paper from the double-sided tape and use the tape to anchor the strips in place.) Continue to add more strips, following the over-and-under weaving process.

4 When the base card is covered and the weaving is complete, neaten off any untidy ends. Run double-sided tape down all four sides of the reverse of the base card and fold the ends of the strips over to hold them in place.

5 Add more double-sided tape to the outer edges of the back of the woven card and attach it to the front of the book to complete the project.

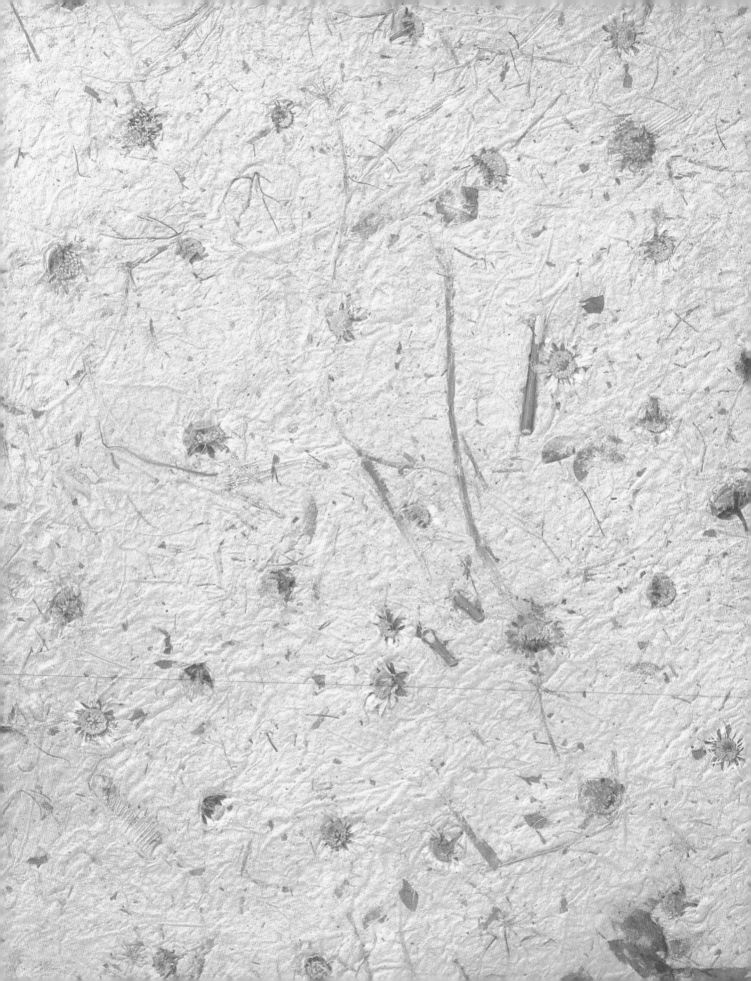

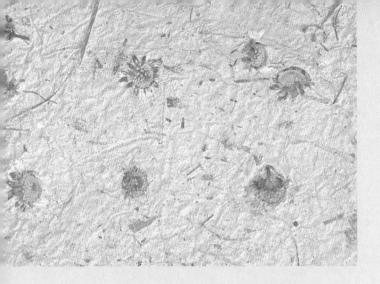

ESSSENTIAL

Templates

In this chapter, you will find all the templates used in the book, plus a few others to inspire you. Page numbers are given when the design is featured in a particular project or variation. Photocopy your chosen template from the book, enlarging it to suit the size of your particular project, and tracing around it.

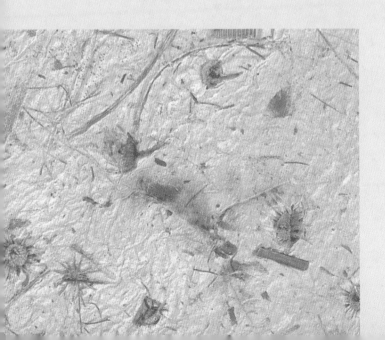

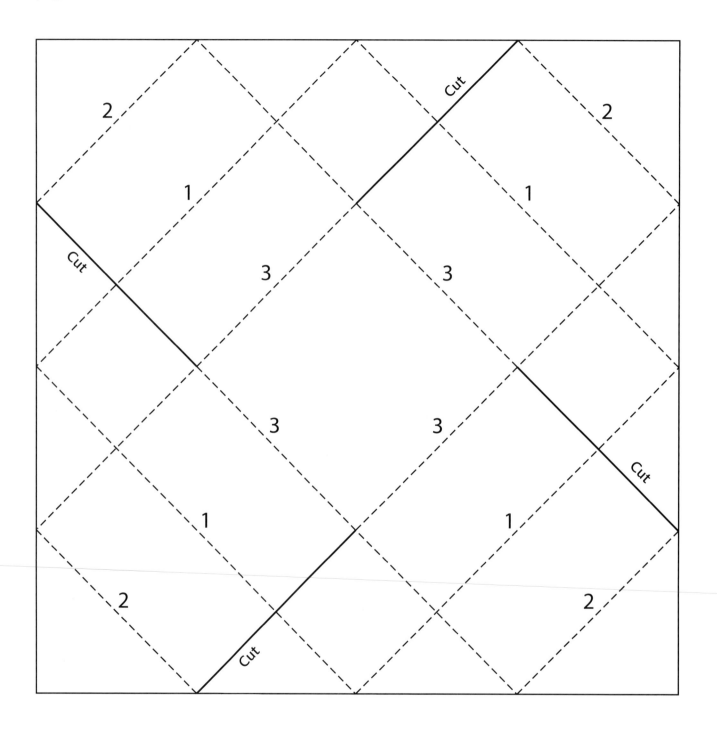

Fold along the dotted lines, following the instructions on pages 38–41. Cut along the solid lines following
the instructions in Steps 5 and 6 on page 40.

Wedding
gift box
page 50

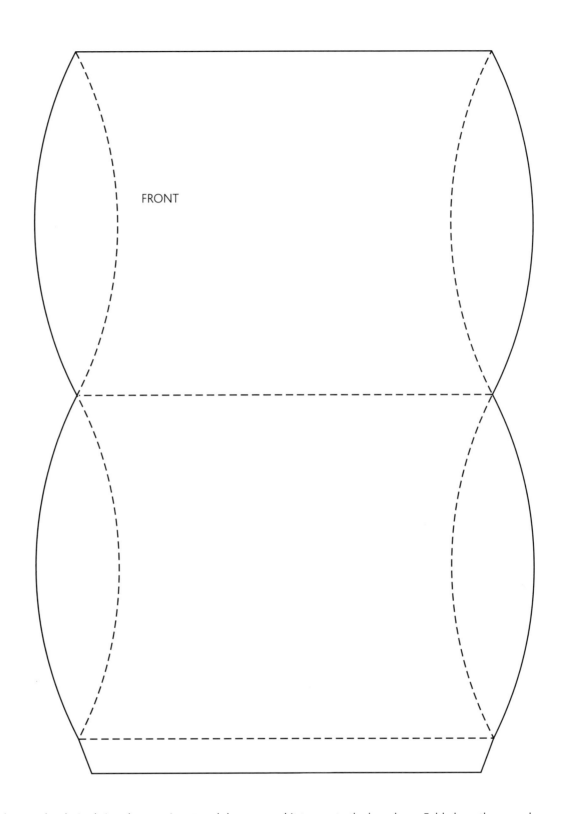

FRONT

Photocopy the template to the desired size, then cut it out and draw around it to create the box shape. Fold along the scored lines, following the instructions on pages 50–52. Make a second template of the front section for use in Step 2.

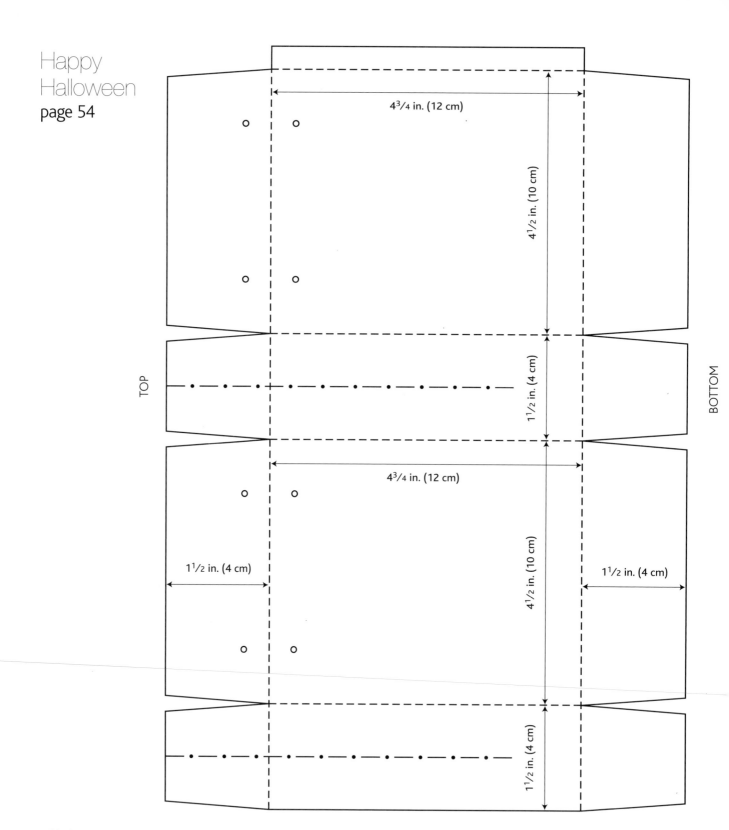

Happy
Halloween
page 54

4³/₄ in. (12 cm)

4¹/₂ in. (10 cm)

TOP

BOTTOM

1¹/₂ in. (4 cm)

4³/₄ in. (12 cm)

1¹/₂ in. (4 cm)

4¹/₂ in. (10 cm)

1¹/₂ in. (4 cm)

1¹/₂ in. (4 cm)

Fold along the dotted lines, following the instructions on page 56. In Step 5,
fold along the two side folds (indicated with lines and dots).

Pretty in pink
page 58

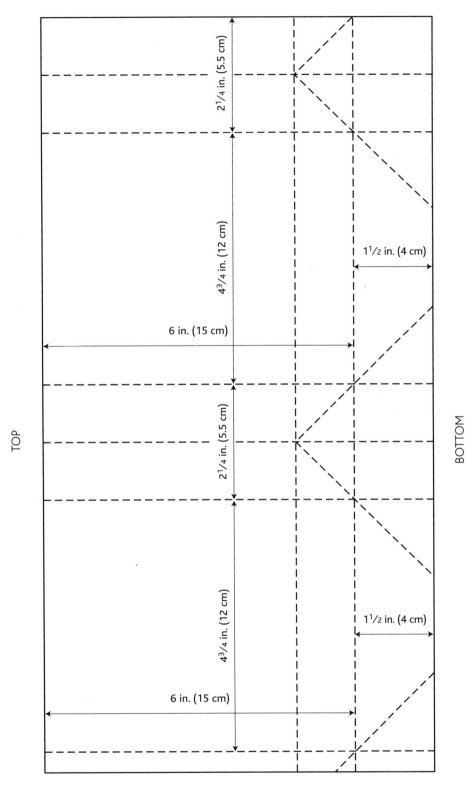

2¼ in. (5.5 cm)

4¾ in. (12 cm)

1½ in. (4 cm)

6 in. (15 cm)

2¼ in. (5.5 cm)

TOP

BOTTOM

4¾ in. (12 cm)

1½ in. (4 cm)

6 in. (15 cm)

Fold along the dotted lines, following the instructions on pages 60–61.

Animal magic and variations
page 82

The templates drawn in a straight, heavy line (below) are to be cut out; those drawn in a light, irregular line (right) are for you to tear out. The project on page 82 features the lion, but you might like to try one of the other animal faces instead.

Photocopy your chosen template, increasing it to the desired size. Cut out all the components of the face, then trace each component onto a relevant shade of paper or cardstock. Cut out the pieces, then reassemble them on the greeting card base using the template as your guide.

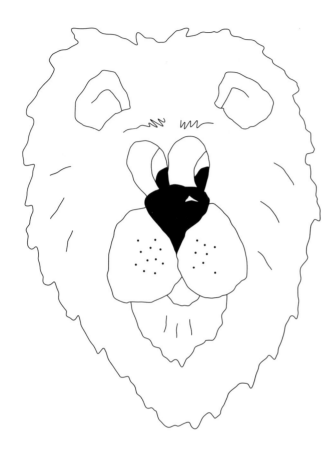

Photocopy your chosen template, increasing it to the desired size. Cut out all the components of the face, then trace each component onto a relevant shade of paper or cardstock. Tear out the pieces by hand, then reassemble them on the greeting card base using the template as your guide.

Animal magic variations

Photocopy your chosen template, increasing it to the desired size. Cut out all the components of the face, then trace each component onto a relevant shade of paper or cardstock. Cut out the pieces, then reassemble them on the greeting card base using the template as your guide.

Photocopy your chosen template, increasing it to
the desired size. Cut out all the components of the
face, then trace each component onto a relevant
shade of paper or cardstock. Tear out the pieces by
hand, then reassemble them on the greeting card
base using the template as your guide.

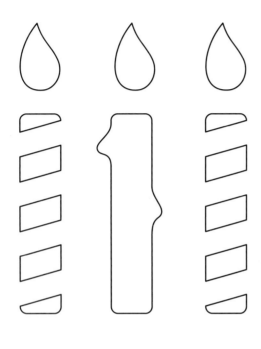

Photocopy your chosen design, then transfer it onto thin cardstock. Do this by using carbon paper or by tracing over the photocopied line with a soft pencil, then rubbing the back of the photocopy with a pencil to transfer the design. Carefully cut out the stencil using a craft knife on a cutting mat.

Be my Valentine and variation
page 92

Fancy frame

page 110

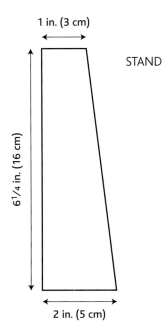

STAND

1 in. (3 cm)

6¼ in. (16 cm)

2 in. (5 cm)

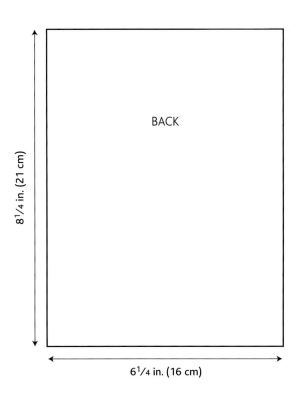

BACK

8¼ in. (21 cm)

6¼ in. (16 cm)

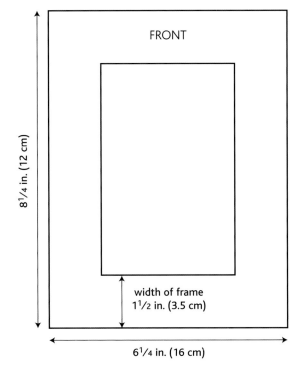

FRONT

8¼ in. (12 cm)

width of frame
1½ in. (3.5 cm)

6¼ in. (16 cm)

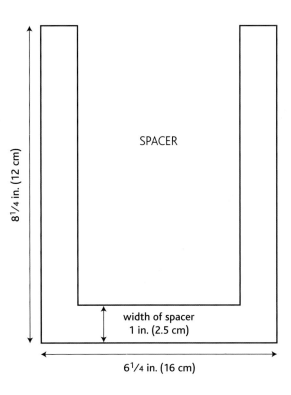

SPACER

8¼ in. (12 cm)

width of spacer
1 in. (2.5 cm)

6¼ in. (16 cm)

Fancy frame variation
page 113

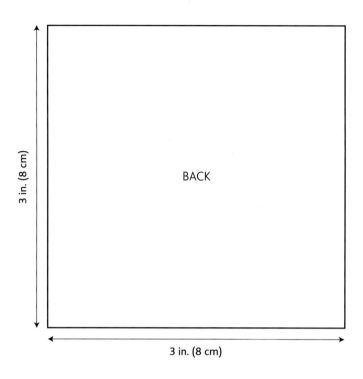

BACK

3 in. (8 cm)

3 in. (8 cm)

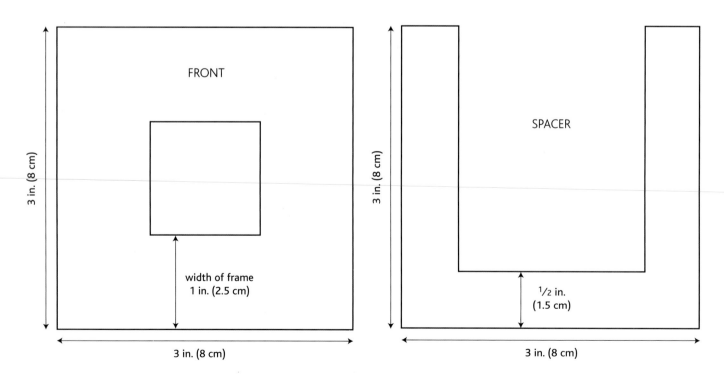

FRONT

width of frame
1 in. (2.5 cm)

3 in. (8 cm)

3 in. (8 cm)

SPACER

¹/₂ in.
(1.5 cm)

3 in. (8 cm)

3 in. (8 cm)

Stationery folder
page 114

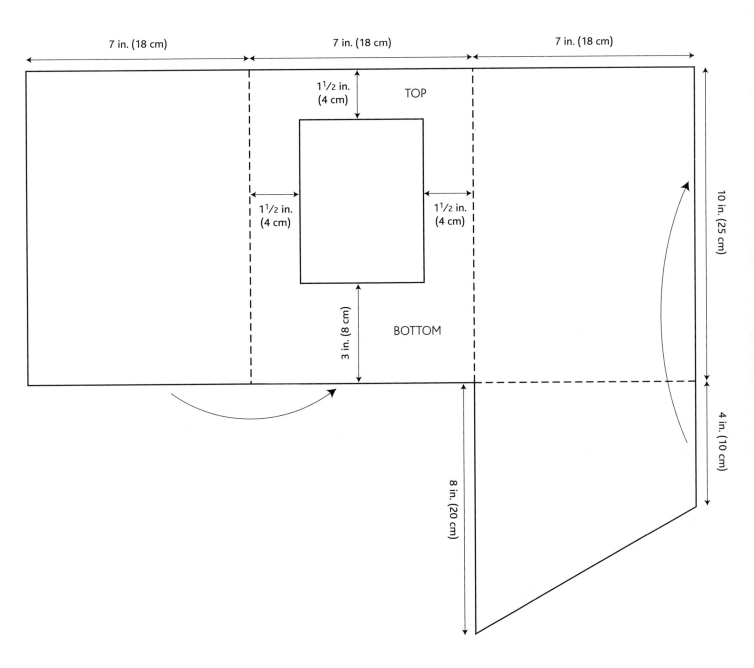

7 in. (18 cm) 7 in. (18 cm) 7 in. (18 cm)

1¹/₂ in. (4 cm)

TOP

1¹/₂ in. (4 cm)   1¹/₂ in. (4 cm)

10 in. (25 cm)

3 in. (8 cm)

BOTTOM

4 in. (10 cm)

8 in. (20 cm)

Fold along the dotted lines, following the instructions on pages 116–18.

Papercut bunting
page 130

Papercut bunting variation
page 131

Papercut bunting variations

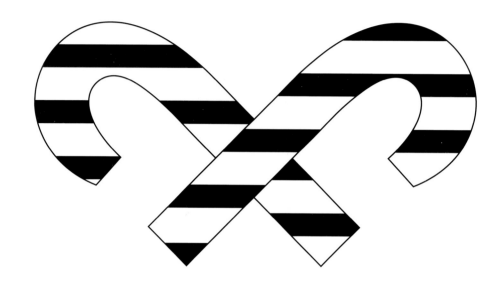

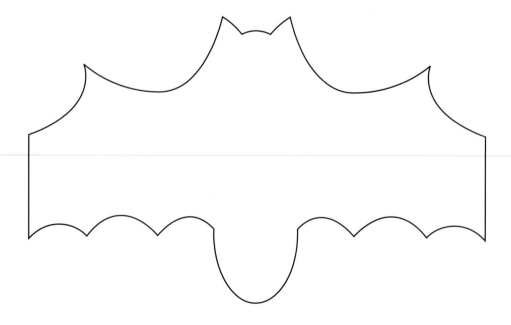

Index

Page numbers in *italics* refer to illustrations. As many papercraft materials and techniques are used throughout the book, the page references are intended to direct the reader to substantial entries only.

Acknowledgments

Breslich & Foss Ltd. and Lynne Garner would like to thank the following individuals for their help in the creation of this book:

Stephen Dew for the templates
Kevin Hart for the illustrations
Helen Huckle for editorial assistance
Clare Louise Hunt for providing additional material
Janet James for designing the book
Janet Ravenscroft for project management
Shona Wood for the photographs